Q:

He **b**roke up with me but hasn't to his **fa**mily (three months) and they still **t**ext me.

A:

It doesn't matter. You want it to matter because you still want him. All it means is that you are no longer in a relationship with a bad communicator.

Q:

Adv **i**ce for first date with a guy way hott**e**r than me?

A:

He wants to go on a date with you. Don't forget that. He can be hot, and a total nightmare. Your job on date one isn't getting the hot guy to like you, it's making sure he can offer you much more than a pretty face before you give him date two.

Q:

I'm i**n** love w/ two guys . . .

A:

No, you're not. You really like two guys and love things about both.

Q:

Hang**ing** out with a guy. WAY more sexua**l** experience than me. Does it matte**r**?

A:

Only if you two are afraid to talk about it.

Don't Text Your Ex Happy Birthday

Don't Text Your Ex Happy Birthday

. . . and other advice on
love, sex, and dating

NICK VIALL

Abrams Image, New York

Editor: Samantha Weiner
Managing Editor: Mike Richards
Designer: Zach Bokhour
Design Manager: Heesang Lee
Production Manager: Rachael Marks

Library of Congress Control Number: 2022933587

ISBN: 978-1-4197-5549-1
eISBN: 978-1-64700-360-9
Signed Edition ISBN: 978-1-4197-6668-8

ABRAMS The Art of Books
195 Broadway, New York, NY 10007
abramsbooks.com

CONTENTS

CHAPTER 1

INTRODUCTION

WHY I WROTE THIS BOOK

This whole book is about being honest with yourself. Despite the title, this book is not really about trying to understand other people—this book is really about understanding yourself, and understanding your choices. It's about getting the outcome that you want in the long term, avoiding the outcome you don't want, and not feeling bad about yourself unnecessarily in the short term. Most of the things I talk about are really just about controlling the things you can control, not giving away the power you do have, and not wasting your mental energy or your time.

Why am I even writing this book? Where am I coming from? I'm always careful to make it very clear that I'm obviously not a trained expert in this type of thing, I am not a therapist or relationship counselor, and I'm not an anthropology professor—I didn't take classes for this. I'm just some guy giving his point of view, which, luckily for me, a lot of people seem to find helpful and interesting.

Everybody knows my dating history from my thirties: I was on TV, pretty obviously totally invested in dating and finding someone, in finding a serious relationship. Since my stint in front of the camera ended, there's a series I do on a weekly basis on Instagram where I get questions from my followers. They're relationship-type questions, and my answers vary from funny one-liners to short explanations. Over the years that evolved into a podcast, where people call in and we talk, and it's more of a long-form advice situation.

A lot of people might wonder—why is this guy talking about dating? Since I've been on dating shows, there's this perception out there about the type of relationships I've been in, or that this dating thing might not ever be a challenging thing for me at all. But I've been engaged twice, been horribly ghosted through lots of breakups that felt like the end of the world, been cheated on by a fiancée, moved in with partners, and moved them out. And I've felt pain and rejection and confusion, I've felt powerless and frustrated, and I've also felt love, real love, healthy love. That's the point of view I'm coming from now—I don't think a lot of people know that. I relate to heartache—and if you don't believe me, skip ahead and check out the whole story of my first terrible heartache on page 179. I want you to know that I understand, and that I really have been through this stuff too.

A lot of other people might also think, why is this straight, white dude telling me how I should act or think? And I recognize that too—there are plenty of people who might feel that way, and to a certain degree, I can't help that, but I do want to talk about it.

Obviously, there are always critics on the internet. When you put stuff out there, it's open for criticism—and that's okay. One person, you know, they referred to me as a reformed fuckboy, just because of the perception of me on TV. They wrote, "Why is this reformed fuckboy telling women and anyone else what they should do better, or how they should act?" She followed that up with, "Why don't you talk to men and tell them to act better?"

And, and my response to that is: Well, I don't have access to the person who's doing you wrong, and I don't know why they're doing it. But I do think I can offer you a couple bits of advice and tools to help control your situation—either you can do something differently and improve the situation you choose to be in, or you can remove yourself from the situation. I can try to help you understand your situation a little bit more honestly.

Literally, every time someone calls or writes in, all I'm doing is trying to get a more honest interpretation of their situation—and I've said this one line all the time—because no one will lie to you more than you will lie to yourself. We all know the biggest liars we will ever meet are ourselves. We're in our heads all the time, lying to ourselves constantly, right? We're rewriting narratives and events because we have egos, and we're often afraid of the truth, or because we're invested in one outcome. And that gets us into these situations, or makes us stay in situations that maybe aren't the best for us. And I'm just trying to give the people asking for my help a very honest point of view.

Many of the questions submitted to me are from women—not exclusively, but that's the majority of my audience. But honestly, I generally believe that most of my advice is really applicable to anyone regardless of your gender or sexual identity. I do want to address the people who read that last sentence with some skepticism: Whoever you are reading this book, I am sure there are many differences between you and me. I can't begin to understand all your struggles, but when it comes to love, dating, and heartbreak, I have experienced many of the fears and disappointments. I have worried about ending up alone, I have been insecure about not being enough, and I have wasted a ton of my time and energy on people who didn't give the same back to me.

In my own life, I ultimately realized that maybe I didn't deserve what happened to me in the past, but I did give that power to other people. I chose to give it to them. I chose to give them the opportunity to hurt or confuse me over and over. I chose to do all that. And I've learned that I need to stop doing that, regardless of what they do, because I can't control what they do. I can only control what I do. I spent a lot of energy trying to figure out how I could change their minds or change their perspectives and change their actions. And I realized that it's a losing battle, and one that also made me feel very powerless. Understanding how to be more honest with yourself and feel more powerful in dating is generally the overall theme of what I talk about online, and in my podcast, and in this book.

A lot of what I'll talk about is very simple in theory, you know—logically, it's not overly complicated, it's that emotional piece that so often messes us up. It might be hard to implement this kind of honesty at first, because it's changing your behavior, and holding yourself accountable to do what you know is best for you—it requires being vulnerable, and opening yourself up to rejection or confrontation. All of those are hard things to do.

Everything I talk about in this book is something that I have to learn the hard way. It took a lot of years and a lot of conversations with myself and my friends—and tears—to figure out what I am sharing with you here. If you're reading this book, chances are you have some kind of struggle with love, relationships, or dating. My hope is that you find a few things that might help make the challenges of love and heartbreak just a little easier.

What follows are the really big concepts that are important to consider in your dating life and when reading this book, and I talk about them over and over in anything I do. Taken together, they'll help make dating less stressful for yourself. And remember that none of this should be taken as a strict set of rules, that you must do exactly this to get exactly that. So much of dating depends on your own situation—so use this book as a guide, not a manual. Like I said, it's all about getting the outcome that you want in the long term, avoiding the outcome you don't want, and learning to stop feeling bad about yourself unnecessarily in the short term.

Remember that you're only looking for one, not many.

I talk to people all the time about dating, and I just hear the frustrations, and those frustrations turn into excuses and reasons to give up, like the belief that there must be something wrong with them, or that all the good ones are taken.

Let's say you are going to build a house: When you're eighteen, you have to start building the house that you're going to live in for the rest of your life. And you can take all the time in the world to build the house. But no matter what, this is your house, and this is the house you have to live in for the rest of your life.

Would you take two weeks to build the house? No, you'd take the time you need to make it the best house, because that's your house. Now just replace the words "your house" with "your relationship." And yet, some people want to find love at first sight, and they don't want to work for it, and they don't want it to be hard, and they want it to just happen. They want people to just show up with an amazing house that's pretty and safe and sturdy. But the more time we put into making sure the foundation's good and the bones are good and the wiring, electricity, and plumbing are good, the safer and prettier and sturdier it'll be.

Dating can be fun. It can be enjoyable if you have the right mindset. You can have some unexpected adventures while dating that you honestly don't fully appreciate until you're not doing it anymore. But, if I'm being honest, it's a bit of a grind and often it's more like working out than having fun. At the gym you can get tired and worn out and fatigued, and sometimes you just need to take a breather and rest. Dating can be the same way, because you're sifting through all the different personalities and people and options that you have, and most of us are trying to find a single person to spend the rest of our lives with, so it can get exhausting. Even those of us who want non-monogamous relationships or even polyamorous ones—we're still usually looking for one or two people with whom to have that core connection.

When you think about it in those terms, dating *should* be somewhat of a challenge. You should honestly want to put in the work, take your time, and do it right. Being in a relationship is not the definition of success when it comes to your love life. It's being in a relationship with the right person for you.

Set your expectations and enforce your boundaries.

In this book I use the terms "expectations" and "boundaries" frequently. Expectations are essentially what you assume you'll get from the other person and the relationship: Are you exclusive? Do you only have casual sex? Do you anticipate hearing from them at least once a day? Is this a one-time thing and if neither of you ever hear from the other person again, that's fine? Those definitions can change over the lifespan of a relationship, but ideally, you'd discuss and define them with the person you're dating or sleeping with. (As I mention in nearly every chapter of this book.)

Boundaries, on the other hand, are the rules you set up for yourself about relationships. Do you not want to be in a sexual relationship with someone who is sleeping with other people? Do you not want to date people who aren't interested in having a serious relationship? Then those are boundaries—you need to set them with yourself, discuss them with the people you date, and then enforce them. And a lot of times, enforcing the boundary means walking away. If a person you're dating says, "Well, I don't do long distance" and you want it to be serious, then you two figure out how to close the distance or you don't keep dating.

Be honest.

The underlying theme of this book, in every interaction, is about being more honest. About who we are, and what we want. And we have to try to be honest with ourselves first, in part so that we can get more honest answers from other people about their intentions and the things that they want. The more honest we are with ourselves about what we really want, the more likely we will get it, or at least not waste time trying to get what won't be given. Do we want to just have sex and watch a movie with someone every once in a while? Do we know we want a long-term relationship and probably shouldn't accept the above?

Being honest with ourselves doesn't mean we'll get everything we want—but there will be less disappointment on both sides, less time spent with people you don't really like, and more likelihood you'll get what you want eventually. Talk through your expectations and boundaries with the person you're dating or hooking up with whenever you're confused or need clarity or wonder if you're on the same page with the feelings. And also look to people's actions versus their words as a gauge of whether or not they're being honest with you when you ask these questions. The goal is just that everyone out there dating be self-aware and accountable. That way, everyone is more honest, so people get hurt less often and enjoy dating more—or at least hate dating less.

Go for grateful over hopeful.

I have realized in recent years that one very helpful way to figure out if any relationship you're in is healthy or toxic—or just worth the effort—is to reflect on two important feelings: gratitude and hope. Figure out how much hope you have for the relationship compared to how much gratitude you have for what you're receiving from the relationship. This is a great way to get the answer of whether you should stay, go, or open up the channels of communication to try to get more of what you want and less of what you don't want.

I began to apply this idea to dating not long ago after my buddy told me to listen to a podcast where a sports writer named Wright Thompson talked about the concept of gratitude—that was the first time I'd heard the idea that gratitude is the only feeling that can't turn toxic. Because gratitude is feeling thankful for what someone or something has given you when they expected nothing in return—like making you feel loved, or listened to. I thought that was a really interesting idea to apply to dating, and the more I thought about it, the more relevant it seemed to be. The basic concept was this idea that most of these emotions we think of as being totally positive in our relationships with other people all have this counter feeling if things don't go the way we want. And when that happens, they turn toxic, and they have a toxic opposite. Love's ugly cousin is hate, enjoyment's ugly cousin is boredom, and hope's ugly cousin is disappointment. Happiness—its toxic cousin is sadness. The toxic cousin of joy: sorrow.

In this way of thinking, true gratitude is being grateful for something that was given without any expectation of something in return—which shouldn't turn into a negative thing. When you're truly grateful for something, it is usually a positive influence on your life. You're grateful that someone makes you feel special and loved, that they make you a priority. These are positive, healthy things.

This stuck with me even more because when people are in relationships, they always talk about their hopes—which are things they wish they could change about their partner or behaviors they could fix, many of which rarely come to fruition. I believe that keeping a grateful versus hopeful list in mind is a good way to keep track of what's important to us in our relationships, and what's really the best for us in the long run.

Know the difference between emotions and an emotional connection.

When you meet someone for the first time and you're attracted to them, there's all kinds of things you like about them. You think they're funny. You like how tall they are. You like that they're polite—you know, she opened the door for me. He paid attention to me. He laughed at my jokes, whatever it is. While all of those things are nice, they're not really an emotional connection.

A real emotional connection can take months or maybe longer, because it begins only when you have built some level of trust, and when you have a level of comfort with how this other person is going to behave around you. A real emotional connection is not wondering how they really feel about you. It's not wondering if they're going to call the next day or worrying that you won't ever hear from them again because you feel like you said something weird. It's knowing they have learned about some of your weaknesses and you still feel connected and safe with them.

A lot of people might say, "What do you mean there's no connection? I feel connected." A lot of people will think, *Oh, I have a connection with someone because I've been dating them consistently for two months.* That's chemistry, that's excitement, and I am sure that's all kinds of emotions, but it's not yet an emotional connection—and I want to make sure you understand the distinction.

Know the difference between pet peeves and non-negotiables.

The difference between pet peeves and non-negotiables is something I learned about when I talked to a behavioral scientist named Logan Ury on my podcast. Logan also wrote a book about relationships and dating—*How to Not Die Alone*—and she had a big chapter about non-negotiables and pet peeves. Logan did not create these concepts, but the way she articulated them with respect to each other really shifted my perspective. Ever since that conversation, I've been using that language myself to describe the difference between annoying things you should be able to live with in an otherwise good relationship (pet peeves), and the things you wouldn't want to live with in any relationship at all (non-negotiables), and I bring both terms up often in this book.

Examples of non-negotiables are not speaking to you with disrespect, anger, or violence. Maybe it's refusing to meet your family, stop sleeping with other people, or move to the city where you live. Some people talk themselves into believing those are annoyances, but they're actually real reasons to leave a relationship.

Examples of pet peeves are that your partner really hates horror movies and won't let you watch them when you're together. That can be annoying. But I always say, "Remember that everyone is annoying." There isn't a single person that doesn't get on someone else's nerves from time to time. Even greatness can be annoying. Hell, that sometimes feels really fucking annoying. For most of us though, our annoying habits aren't tied to greatness; they're just run-of-the-mill everyday stupid shit that we do that gets on other people's nerves. We all have annoying habits. Maybe we all try to hide them as much as we can, but we are who we are. Those are usually just pet peeves.

Instead of panicking when you come across behaviors you don't like, you have to figure out what's really important to you in a relationship. When someone annoys you, is that a non-negotiable or a pet peeve? It's an exercise in trying to figure out how much of a big deal someone's undesirable behavior is to you. If you're thinking, *I really like a lot of other things about this person beyond this annoying thing they do,* that's okay. Or maybe you make a list of things you hope to change and things you're grateful for and you realize that annoying thing is on a long list of things you hope to change, next to a short list of things about the person you're grateful for.

Take me for example: I leave cupboard doors open. I leave clean laundry piled up. In other words, I'm slightly messy. And I know it's super irritating to live with someone like that. Most of the time it's something my girlfriend, Natalie, teases me about, and we laugh, and sometimes it actually gets annoying for her. I hate that I do it, and I try to remember not to do it because I don't want to be a nuisance to her, but whatever, sometimes I can't help it. It's not a non-negotiable for her because there's a difference between accidentally being messy and not feeling loved or appreciated.

Messy is one thing, but let's pay more attention to how someone treats you and how they communicate and how they deal with disappointment. That deserves more weight than how good they are at folding laundry.

Get comfortable with being single.

This might sound corny or like a cliché, but maybe the most important thing of all is that you need to be comfortable with being single—maybe even more to the point, you need to be comfortable being alone. And part of that is being confident that "single" is not some bad word, some sort of scarlet letter you need to explain or justify to your friends and family. There's a challenge there, not just because of your own feelings or insecurities, but because in almost every culture and in our society, you get to a certain age, and your family members will start asking, "Why are you still single?" As if you're doing something wrong. Facing those expectations can be a challenge—and I know women deal with it even more than men do.

Getting comfortable with being single was not an easy concept for me, not at first.

My twenties, for the most part, consisted of three long and serious monogamous relationships with women I thought I would marry, and I didn't do a lot of dating in between. When I was single, I felt like I was incomplete, and I put a lot of pressure on myself to have a partner. I had these expectations in my twenties of having a relationship just like my parents—who still love each other, and who met in their early twenties and started having kids right away, and et cetera, et cetera, et cetera.

When my first relationship didn't work out and I found myself at the age my parents were when they met and married, I made a bad situation worse by thinking less of myself for this perceived failure. I had never been in love before that first relationship. I really didn't know how to get over her, even though my first relationship was one of those youthful, toxic-type relationships where we broke up and got back together over and over and over. No matter what, it's kind of scary after your first real breakup—how do you get over your first love? You literally don't know that you can love someone else when you're at that stage in your life—you've never even felt love before this. So you don't know if you'll ever feel that kind of love again.

As a result, I was desperate to find someone, anyone. I can tell you from experience that you're more prone to jumping into relationships that aren't healthy when you're desperate to find someone. When I met a girl who was just so different than my previous girlfriend, that was the part I fell in love with. That's a common story—we do that a lot, right? I fell in love with the idea of a person, because she was the opposite of someone who had hurt me. It was purely reactionary.

When we started dating, I just ignored that everything I was learning about her was evidence of just how incompatible we really were. I was determined to make it work, because in my mind, I was like, I can't have this not work—I have to find a person now. We got engaged—and then she cheated on me.

When my first serious relationship ended, I didn't know if I could get over it. When my second serious girlfriend cheated on me, it was so painful, I couldn't help but feel like I was somehow inadequate. But after my third serious relationship ended—she was great, but we were just incompatible for the long haul—I finally realized that the breakup wasn't proof that I was somehow less than. I knew I would get over it. In fact, I was the one who broke it off.

After that, I didn't get another serious girlfriend for years. I dated a ton, and I met a lot of great women. I was okay with being single. I met more people and I took more risks—I moved to a different city, I invested more in myself and my career. And so the next time I met somebody I sparked with, instead of shying away from potential disappointment, I found myself asking more important questions about who they were and what they wanted in life and a relationship, because I genuinely wanted to find out. I was finally comfortable being myself and taking things slowly.

But what had also happened was that I had a talk with my grandma after the second of my first two big breakups. I was about twenty-eight at that point, and as I said, I thought I would marry each of those girlfriends, so I wasn't where I thought I would be. I was heartbroken. My friends tried to make me feel better, talk me out of my despair, and my parents were worried. But I remember it was my grandma Phyllis who sat me down and taught me something I've never forgotten.

She said to me, "You know what your problem is? You have no perspective. You're so young, you have so much to learn." Now it is, of course! But at that time, I thought to myself, *Oh my God, why? Why do I have to learn any more?* I didn't agree with her. But how could I tell my eighty-year-old grandma she didn't know what she was talking about? So instead, I listened. And then she talked about all the things that happened in her own life at various stages, and how she lived through them, including getting divorced from my grandpa in the 1970s when that was still rare, when she still had five kids to raise as a single mother. So yeah, she had perspective that I didn't have.

She was the first person who told me that I would grow, learn, live, have other loves, and someday look back and see how what I thought was the end of the world wasn't even the beginning. That eventually I'd also get some perspective about my heartbreak. The thought that I'd one day look back on that point from a place of happiness never crossed my mind as a young man with a bruised ego—at that age you kind of just think the world revolves around you, and you can't imagine what it is like to be any older.

Have you ever heard the saying that every day you wake up and it's the oldest you've ever been? Think about that for a minute. When you're really young, you lack any perspective at all—you don't have a lot of dating experience to look back on, like you do when you're thirty or forty-five or even twenty-nine. When you're a teen, twenty-five seems like a big deal. It's old. Thinking about what I know now versus what I knew when I was sixteen or seventeen—that's really hard for a young person to imagine. But as you get older, you develop the self-awareness to say, "You know, one day I'll be thirty or forty-five or sixty, and there's a whole lot more I have left to do and see and learn."

Essentially, my grandma Phyllis taught me that one day I'd meet the right person, and I'd be fine, however long it took. At twenty-five, I was thinking, *Well, I don't want to wait too long to find somebody. I want it now.* But she taught me to approach my love life, my romantic life, like I had time, a lot of life left to live. That I had time to be patient for the right person.

And I think that is relatable for a lot of young people. Those first heartbreaks were my first real loves. I even proposed to one of those women. With your early loves, you often talk about your future a lot, you play house a lot. You think, *Oh, we love each other. I guess we should talk about questions like: What if we want to get married? Do we want to have kids?* Thinking about love, thinking about marriage, talking about weddings, and talking about who we'd invite and what we'd do.

And then, you know, the relationship doesn't work out. But just as my grandmother told me, I made my peace with that. I finally got to a point where I was, *Wow, I'm thankful it didn't work out.* I went from being sad and heartbroken that the relationship ended to being thankful it did. I got that perspective. I got okay with being single—I embraced the waiting, and I started to enjoy my time.

When you're single, you don't have to worry about sacrifices. You can be selfish with your time, you can meet multiple people. You can be spontaneous and do things on the spur of the moment without taking anyone else into account. You don't have to check in. You can randomly DM someone, and there's a lot of freedom in that. Try to embrace it and stop worrying about why your friends are asking why you haven't found someone yet, and stop worrying about the societal pressures from your family or even the pressure in your own head. Now, when someone asks why haven't you found your person yet, you can just say, "I just haven't found anyone worthy of my time."

Don't sweat the timeline.

By the time I got into my thirties, I was so happy being single, I remember there was a little bit of a pivot from my parents. At first, my parents were more worried about me being sad and heartbroken. They'd say to me, "You'll be okay. It's okay to be single. Enjoy this time in your life." They had to try to convince me of that. But then I could tell that there was some anxiousness on their part as I approached and then passed age thirty. Then it became, "Oh, Nick, when are you going to settle down?" Because I was totally single there for a couple of years, and totally comfortable with my single life.

At a certain point my mom was like, "You know, Nick, maybe start thinking about getting a girlfriend again?" And I just remember saying to her: "Mom, look, I've had these big breakups and big relationships, and now I'm just really comfortable with being patient." And then I said, "You know, I don't know when I'm going to find my person, but I would rather find them when I'm forty-two and be with them and have a great marriage for as long as I live—which hopefully might be another thirty, forty years—than be married and divorced at thirty-nine after a three-year marriage that failed."

Like I said, you have to remember that you're only looking for one, not many.

I don't want to wait till I'm forty-five to get married, but I'm *willing* to wait till I'm forty-five—and not panic and not force it, because I have the rest of my life to enjoy that person. That's why I want to make sure that I'm with the right person, rather than be so impatient that I put an arbitrary timeline on my dating life.

It starts with someone saying something like, "Well, he gets really mad and he calls me terrible names that make me cry, but I know he doesn't mean it"—because what is really in the back of your mind is, *If I break up with this person, I have to start over. This time will all have been wasted. Time I can't get back.* That person will stay in that relationship because they've told themselves they have to be married by thirty, and they're twenty-nine, and this relationship is already three years old. They'll think to themselves, *I just don't have it in me to start all over again.* Most of the time people will tell themselves, *You know what? I'm just going to lean into this thing.*

But someone who makes you feel bad about yourself is a non-negotiable—being talked to in a demeaning way that you're not okay with is a non-negotiable. Maybe you've tried to talk to them about it. Maybe they say they're going to work on it. But they never do, and you realize that's just who they are. It sucks that it took that long to figure it out, but isn't that better than sticking around and dealing with that for forty more years? Hopefully you'll live until you are eighty or ninety—think about what it would be like to be in a marriage that long with someone that you've already realized doesn't make you feel good about yourself.

It is kind of nuts when you spell it out like that, yet so many people do that. So many people will knowingly commit to something that will give them a lifetime of pain, just for the fleeting feeling of having "succeeded" at love.

I do realize that, as a man, I haven't had to face the ticking of my biological clock the way women who want children do, and I can only imagine that it must be a powerful force. But I do believe the bigger picture is that both men and women—everyone—put these deadlines in our heads. We'll think only about the timeline, and then we'll start compromising on what we're looking for in a relationship that should be the best thing in our lives. True success in love is found by refusing to settle.

Meet your ego.

The heart of this book is about being able to better control what you can control in dating and relationships—and often in dating situations it's really our ego making the decisions. Once we're aware, we can stop letting that happen. The first time I met my ego was when I was cheated on in my early twenties by my fiancée. I had all these negative thoughts when I first found out, all this pride and indignation—I couldn't believe that I would be cheated on, and I couldn't believe I got engaged only to get cheated on; I never imagined this for myself. All of which I came to realize were ego-driven feelings, not the feelings of getting over an actual heartbreak. That moment in my life is me meeting my ego for the first time, acknowledging that I had one, and recognizing the role my ego played in my actions.

Up until that point, I didn't have any self-awareness about my ego; in fact I am pretty sure that if someone had told me, "Oh, you have an ego," I probably would have been defensive, "No way!" Because I would have been thinking of it in terms of somebody with the biggest ego in the world. But after that breakup, I thought to myself, *Of course I have an ego. We all have egos.* I spent a lot of time thinking about what that meant and how many of my choices, especially when it came to that specific heartbreak, weren't about my feelings toward her or the relationship, but what this breakup or being cheated on said about me —and also what other people would think about me.

I remember a moment—so vividly—of being out at this bar at that time in my life. I was finally getting back out there, but I still wasn't totally healed. I remember someone asking me, "What happened? Why did you break up?" And I was just like, "Oh, you know, it just ended." I was really ashamed. I was embarrassed about acknowledging that I got cheated on, because I felt like it said something about me. Which is, I think, a very common feeling that many people deal with in relationships when the other person does something that hurt us. We spend a lot of time trying to not feel less than, which is essentially fighting with our egos.

I was thinking those exact thoughts, and then I had this realization: *Wait, why am I embarrassed about this? What did I do?* The next time I went out and someone asked me that question—"What happened?"—I just said, very matter factly, "Oh, she cheated on me." And the response I got was, "Well, that was shitty of her." I didn't feel embarrassed, and the person I talked to didn't look upon me with any judgment, either.

With many relationship decisions, we're thinking about what society is going to think about us, or what people are going to say about us. That's ego, and ego can lead us to bad decisions. Ego gets in the way of our ability to heal, and to move on from bad or hurtful situations. Our egos also often delay the process of removing ourselves from a relationship that we know deep down isn't where it should be, and even can be what make us chase people that we already know aren't good for us.

Just the other day I was asked, "Why do I keep making the same mistakes over and over by dating jerks? What's the best way to meet a nice person? And my answer was: "By not chasing validation." What I meant was, it's not that you're only attracting jerks. It's that your ego is searching for validation, and that feeling of being special. You ego says, "I want to find the person who treated everyone else with disrespect, but treated me like a queen, because I was the special one."

Ego is often what's at play when we give so many second chances to people who give us so many reasons why they don't deserve our time. Whether it's the fuckboy or the player I talk about later in the book (page 39), they are the people who constantly shower us with disappointments. Why do we keep giving these people so many chances? It's not because they're sophisticated narcissists who could teach a master class in manipulation and we're at the mercy of their mind control. That's not the reason—it's often because our egos want to feel special and validated.

That's why I want anyone reading this book to take some time and meet their ego, and really think about their ego in every choice they make in dating and in a relationship. *Am I doing this because it's going to make my heart happy, and make me feel loved and cared for—or am I doing this for my ego?* And if you choose to prioritize being happy with every decision you make about your relationships, and even in life in general, you're going to be far better off.

QUESTIONS WITH NICK

Q:

Married & cheated on 2x. Staying and working on it. Does that make me stupid or loyal?

A:

It makes you loyal, vulnerable, and scared. Not stupid. But just don't think you can't live without them . . . and know that you deserve better.

Q:

Do I stay friends with a guy who I dated for 5 years but broke up with because he cheated?

A:

Not if you really want to move on and make yourself available for the person who is worth your time.

QUESTIONS WITH NICK

Q:

Do you consider yourself to be ruled by your ego or your soul?

A:

That never ending struggle is what life is all about and perfecting your life is based on the strength of the soul over the ego.

Q:

Why is my ego bruised by someone I don't even like?

A:

Your ego doesn't care what you like, it just cares about how special it feels.

Q:

Advice for being the only single one out of all your friends

A:

Grass is always greener on the other side. You want their life and they miss yours.

CHAPTER 2

TRAINING OUR PICKERS

WHAT'S A PICKER?

Yes, dating is hard, and there are so many things about it that are beyond our control, which is why it makes it so important to control what we can: our choices, our decisions, our communication, and the dates we go on and the people we agree to go on them with. That means refining our pickers. Your picker is the part of your brain—call it a muscle, or tool, if you want—that we use to evaluate who we are going to date, who we are going to invest more time in.

I started using that term by accident, but then I grew to embrace it. I told somebody on a podcast once, "You know, you just have a really bad picker and what you need to do is adjust it." I was trying to make that person feel better, in the sense that just because they have a broken tool, that doesn't mean they are broken.

I compared it to a speedometer in your car—it's broken or off by twenty miles per hour, but that's okay, because all we need to do is adjust it. It's a good analogy because it's just a little part of the car, one of a million pieces that make the car work. A broken speedometer can cause a lot of potential problems—you can get speeding tickets, get into accidents. But it's also not that hard to fix, you know what I'm saying? You don't have to get a whole new engine. You don't have to throw away your car. You don't have to totally start over. So yeah, maybe you had some bad luck and your ex was toxic and they really screwed you over, but instead of focusing on them, let's work on you and your picker for the next time. Let's look at how you choose who you continue to see or spend time with.

And pickers do need to be trained. Like a new puppy, if untrained, our pickers will tend to chase anything exciting regardless of whether it's safe or not. I don't know how many studies out there have been done about picker development (likely none) and when it begins, but if I had to guess I would say it starts at a very early age, probably when we started picking friends in grade school and figured out what kinds of people we were drawn to. By the time we start dating, that picker has accrued some knowledge about the best choices for our romantic investments. It's collected data from how we were raised by our parents, things we learned in school, and our time on the playground. These formative experiences all taught us lessons that trained our pickers in how to choose friends, roommates, mentors. But when you throw the feelings of romance into the equation—that's when things become a bit murkier. To throw another metaphor at you, the picker needs some major tuning to deal with this stage in life, the same way a guitar would if someone played around with all of the strings.

Success early on in dating usually has much more to do with luck than with skill. Sometimes our pickers do win the jackpot without any training or tuning—their first choice is amazing. In a perfect world, every time we lost at picking, we would learn a lesson or two that gave us information to help us make smarter picks the next time. Except the world's not perfect. While some of us do learn over time, "love" usually tends to make us stupid, or at least irrational. Then we ask our friends to help us with our pickers, but they are often as dumb as we are, so it's just one untrained picker giving advice to another.

The point is that we do get to pick who we spend time with—most of us no longer live in a society where our parents tell us who we're supposed to marry. It's important to remember that truth when we sometimes feel like things aren't going our way and things don't feel fair and we've had a string of bad dates or we didn't see sparks fly. When we say things like "I don't know why I can't find anyone," that's when it's important to remember that we are in some control of our dating lives. It might not always work out exactly how we planned. It doesn't mean we won't be disappointed by others. But we will always get to choose who we invest our time and energy in. So we should do our best to pick as well as we can.

So, I figured I would make some notes on how to train your pickers, things I've learned not just from dating, but from hearing about lots of other bad picks. And one of the most important things your picker can do is learn to recognize the fuckboys (or fuckgirls, or really fuckpeople) and players in your life as soon as possible. These are the two main types of people on whom you will waste the most time and emotional energy while you are dating. If you can avoid them, or avoid spending too much time on them, you avoid disappointment—or worse, real emotional pain.

WHAT IS A FUCKBOY, ANYWAY?

I've said it before, and I'll say it again: Anyone can be a fuckboy (I'll be using that term throughout, regardless of gender, because, if we're being honest, I think we all know that fuckboy really refers to a state of mind). While maybe most fuckboys are men (given their propensity to more easily detach emotionally from sex), women can also be considered fuckboys, LGBTQIA people can be fuckboys. Frankly, everyone has the potential to be a fuckboy. As such, it's 100 percent certain that we will encounter them while we're out braving the dating world, and likely very often. First, you have to realize one person's fuckboy is another's future life partner. A fuckboy is someone you're dating casually or someone you're having sex with who is just not that interested in you. Fuckboys are not usually bad people—though they are normally the one in the relationship receiving more affection, attention, and dedication than they're giving. Fuckboys tend to have a desire to create and sustain a committed relationship in theory, but in practice they are also willing to have a multitude of casual (to them) dating situations or hookups until they eventually find "the one." Which, to be clear, is not you, if you're in a fuckboy situation.

That's all it really takes to feel like you've been fuckboyed: To want more with someone you've been casually hooking up with.

The reason fuckboys are fuckboys is that they're bad at establishing expectations with intimate partners up front, and this can be for all kinds of reasons. They don't say, "I just want sex," or "I just want someone to occasionally watch a movie with and then have sex with because I am lonely," because they are afraid of disappointing the other person, or afraid of not getting the thing that they want, which is good sex or someone to hang out with. Or maybe they do enjoy the time they spend with you and aren't sure what they want themselves. Hookup culture (page 127) is more prevalent than ever before. With our heads buried in our phones and TikTok on the rise, the art of conversation and communication is in sharp decline. As a result, you're going to have even more encounters with fuckboys.

A classic fuckboy situation is: We had sex. We hung out. I liked you, but you didn't want to commit to anything more. And then, ultimately, it ended. Later, once time passed, you realized, *Oh that was a fuckboy!* But at the time, you were busy trying to figure out the why.

When you don't have the labels of "boyfriend" or "girlfriend" but you hang out and have sex, when you suspect somebody likes you more than you liked them, if you were engaging in sex and someone told you they liked you more than you like them, yet you continue to participate—these are all fuckboy situations. Maybe one of the parties attempted to set boundaries, but they didn't have the determination or fortitude or strength to enforce that boundary, and then you both continue to do the same thing as before—usually that is sex—and then one person becomes the fuckboy. Maybe they listened, maybe they're not totally to blame. Maybe one person said, "I want to date you"—and you said no. Then they say, "Do you want to come over," and you say, "Okay." Someone tried to set a boundary then did a bad job of maintaining it, and so did the other person, even though they agreed to it originally. Even though they knew the boundary was important. But that's a fuckboy quality, not respecting the boundary. And the person being fuckboyed often doesn't respect the boundary either because they wrongly see the broken boundary as a sign that the fuckboy is changing for them.

If you know me, you know I am honest to a fault, sometimes too honest. But I guarantee that if you surveyed every woman I dated or hooked up with, I promise there is somebody who thinks of me as a fuckboy. Maybe I wasn't as clear as I thought, or they weren't listening; maybe things got messy and complicated; maybe we both had our reasons to ignore boundaries, maybe the most righteous version of me would have said "No, we shouldn't do that," but then we did it.

A lot of what happens with fuckboys is just miscommunication about expectations and boundaries. Look at what we call ghosting, or what ghosting means now. "Ghosting" was originally used to describe a situation where someone totally peaced out on you—someone you had some kind of a relationship with, maybe even two or three dates. You had a reasonable expectation to hear from them again, and then they just disappeared. But now ghosting has grown to describe a situation where someone goes on one date with you and there's no follow-up, and you feel bad about it. But that's not ghosting—it is bad communication and being a fuckboy. Maybe that person was avoiding a conversation about their real intentions, or afraid of any kind of conflict, or maybe there were unreasonable expectations about what one date means to both parties.

I am sure on some level this type of behavior has been going on forever, but only until recently has it become so mainstream. I'm pretty sure one of the reasons is increased access to many more potential partners. I for one am thrilled that we aren't limited to our smaller immediate communities when it comes to finding one person to spend the rest of our lives with. I'm glad we are becoming more patient when it comes to finding our person, and not just getting engaged to someone we really like when we're twenty-three years old. There is no denying that social media and dating apps have drastically increased our options (even if it's doesn't always feel that way). But this does create a paralysis of choice: It's like scrolling through Netflix trying to find something to watch—we all have thousands more options than we had just a few years ago.

My whole point of the fuckboy conversation is that now we're all kind of fuckboys at one point or another, because we've become sloppy communicators when we're dating, especially when we're actively participating in hookup culture.

But then, there are the players.

Players are the pigs. Players don't respect the people they date at all. They have no interest in looking for, let alone committing to, a relationship. This is why it's unsurprising that most players are single. Occasionally, players might have a girlfriend or boyfriend, but they have no interest in ever being faithful. They are willing to lie and cheat—instead of just being honest and breaking up—maybe because of their inherent insecurity around being alone. Players prioritize sleeping with as many people as possible, constantly adding to their list of sexual partners. They view sexual partners as conquests.

Players really do have ulterior motives. They want to lead people on. They want to make you think they want to be there. There's no empathy for you—they'll promise to be exclusive with you, and they'll lie to you.

They'll give gifts on birthdays to purposefully make you feel that they are thinking about you and think you're special when they literally don't care about you at all. A player wants you to think that they're the only person in the world, and they will manipulate you to keep you thinking that.

IDENTIFYING FUCKBOYS AND PLAYERS: A GUIDE

Below are the clear signs of fuckboys and players—basically these are signs of anyone who you should avoid. To some degree, it doesn't matter the vernacular that society uses, or what names we call these archetypes. In real life, there are shades of gray, but I don't think it makes that much of a difference in the long run, because it's really about avoiding people who have these behaviors, who aren't giving us what we want in the situation.

It's always about identifying what we want: Do we want a real relationship? Do we want to find one person to commit to? I am trying to help you take a look at yourself and what you want—it's always about looking at our actions and ourselves—and figure out what you can control. And one thing you can control is leaving fuckboys or players behind once you realize that is who they are, or getting better at managing your expectations and boundaries if you decide to keep seeing them.

To that end, your picker should always consider these red flags. When they happen, accept them at face value. Don't try to find a different way to interpret them that is more in line with your dreams and less in line with reality.

FOUR TRAITS OF THE FUCKBOY

 They are inconsistent.

Nothing is a better indicator of someone's lack of excitement about you than if they are inconsistent. Inconsistent with how they show affection, inconsistent with how much you hear from them, inconsistent with their expectations for you. Think about how you treat things when you kind of like them. You enjoy them from time to time, they are better than nothing, but you can live without them—and often do. Anything you're excited about you can't wait to enjoy. It doesn't matter if it's a new person in your life or the amazing new massage therapist. Inconsistency can be normal and often happens in the very early stages of a dating situation—especially when you're still communicating via a dating app—but the more time we spend with someone, the more consistent that time spent hanging out should become, if they are excited. If they continue to be inconsistent, or worse, become more inconsistent than they were before, then there is a solid chance you're being strung along until they find something they think is better.

I don't care what excuses you tell yourself as to why. Their lack of consistency means that they aren't invested. When you're having sex with someone and that person isn't willing to make you a priority, you're interacting with a fuckboy. It shouldn't matter how focused they are on their career right now, or how recently they've gotten divorced. If they're excited about you, they will focus on you. "Nick, what about long distance? That's a reason for someone to be inconsistent." Nope! When we are interested in someone, we make crazy ass exceptions to reasonably acceptable behavior. People who are inconsistent are not excited about you. If you are having sex with someone that you are excited about, but they are not excited about you, it almost certainly means you're falling for a fuckboy.

2 They don't make plans in advance.

Don't hang out with anyone you're interested in romantically who is not willing to make plans with you at least a day in advance. Now, this is more of a guideline, it isn't to be taken so literally, but use your common sense. I mean if Hot Ben, who you had an okay first date with three days ago that left you feeling unsure if there would be a second date, reaches out and says he has tickets to an exciting event, well shit, you go on that date. If Hot Ben sends you a text at three in the afternoon three days after the first date, and that conversation goes something like this:

Hot Ben: Hey, what are you up to later

You: Hi!! Not too much HBU??

Hot Ben: No plans . . . If you're not doing anything later let's grab a drink

Well, just know that Hot Ben was bored. He wanted to do something and you were an option. Again, this is common and okay early on. Sometimes it takes a few strikes of the match before you get any sparks. When it happens on the regular or still after a few dates, then they are flat out not excited about you yet. Now, it's possible they have reservations about investing more time with you, but people who want to see if a relationship is still possible typically address those reservations by getting to know you better. If they never want to make plans ahead of time, then there is an extremely high chance you're just an option to them.

What does it mean when someone agrees to go on a date you planned in advance, but doesn't go out of their way to plan anything on their own? It means they are willing to show up. Now, depending on the situation or how long you've known them, that low-level commitment can be good or bad.

Let's say you've gone on a few dates with the same person. You've had a pretty good time. You're excited about them, but you can never really tell if you two are on the same page. When you think about it, you realize you're probably reaching out to them more than they are reaching out to you. They will say things like, "We should hang out again sometime" or "I might be free next week to hang," but they never say, "I know a great restaurant that I want to take you to this weekend." Well, then you know they aren't that excited about you. They like you enough that they don't mind spending time with you when they have nothing better to do. In other words, you are just an option to this person.

I know what you're thinking—*Not everyone is a planner!* That is very true. I am not a planner. I fucking hate planning, but I do take great pride in people's ability to count on me. So I may not be a good planner, but if I say I'm going to do something, you can count on me to show up. Another thing to remember about this is that even bad planners will plan something when they are excited about it. I often have no idea what I'm doing for dinner let alone a few weeks from now, but when it comes to being excited about going on a date with a woman I really like, you better believe I'm trying to make plans to see her in the near future. Now, the plan still might not have all the polish that it would if it was coming from a skilled and detailed planner, but the effort will be there.

Even if it's the simple gesture of asking if you want to get together tomorrow, at least that shows they are thinking of you ahead of time. You're on their mind. The further in advance they make plans, probably the more excited they are. And if they do make plans, but they are plans that don't show much effort or thought about you, then you're probably dealing with someone who hasn't decided yet whether they want to invest that extra energy in you.

And yes, spontaneity can be fun, but spontaneity should always be followed up with a plan to see you again. A fuckboy is a person who you only hear from because they are bored, horny, or both. Once in a while, these people will seem to be making plans with you, but usually it's only because they are going to a planned event and want to make sure they have a date, or don't want to do something alone. If someone is rarely willing to make a plan at least a day in advance, they are rarely thinking about the relationship. And even when they do think about it, they are not excited. As I said, to them you are an option. Due to dating apps and the ability to match with and message multiple people simultaneously, our options are only increasing. Eventually, you need to stop being an option to people and see who's willing to make you their choice.

If someone constantly agrees to plans and then changes them last minute, always shows up late, or is generally inconsiderate of your time, that's when you can assume they aren't reliable—and also that they aren't that excited or invested in you. I'll add that a common follow-up question I get when I talk about this kind of thing is, "What about the people who make plans with you, but then don't show up?" To which I would reply, "Well, you're dealing with a special type of selfish person who is self-aware enough to know that people like plans, but is still a selfish person. If someone does that to you, walk away."

Last but not least, be reasonable and practical about your expectations—a first date, you know, it's kind of weird to expect someone to make an extravagant plan. If you're going around turning down dates with people who are unwilling to make a grand plan on a first date, well, you might be closing a lot of doors and windows to someone out there with the same amount of options as you have, and the same amount of questions as you have, who just wants to get to know you a little more. But if you're on a second or third date, or you're talking on a regular basis, or if you've been intimate—then it's reasonable to expect someone to plan a date.

3 They always make excuses as to why they don't want a relationship with you.

This should be an obvious way to spot a fuckboy, given that they don't want to advance the relationship with you. Except, for so many of us, even after hearing the excuses, we find ways to misinterpret or just flat-out ignore the signs that we are dealing with a fuckboy.

These excuses can be expressed in many different ways, but it almost always includes "I like you, but . . ." Some assholes will even say "I love you, but . . ."

They are literally telling you they don't want to date you. It doesn't matter at all whether it's preceded with compliments, lots of requests for hookups are followed with "maybe in the future." It really almost doesn't matter what comes after the "but"—*but you live in Oregon; but you are ten years older.* They don't want to date you now, and, to be honest, they never will. Fuckboys will always bring up a reason they can't be in a relationship, but don't ever end the current situation or offer a solution to change it. So don't let your bruised ego stop you from hearing a fuckboy admit what they are to you. Your ego is wrong.

This is why unless you're really good at setting expectations with people you're dating or having sex with (see page 128), almost everyone's a fuckboy. Everyone is a fuckboy until they meet that someone they're willing to make sacrifices for. You can hear it now: "I used to say I didn't want a relationship. And then I met you and, fuck, I'll do anything to be with you. I want to be with you. I want to give up my free time with my friends. I don't care if you live in Oregon. I don't care if you're ten years older." If you're interested in being with someone—voilà, you're not a fuckboy—you make it work.

4 They usually tell you the truth.

The thing is, more often than not, fuckboys will tell you what they are: People who just aren't looking for anything serious right now. For some reason many of us have no problem lying to ourselves and then lying to them and saying "Same" when we actually really want something serious. In reality, we just want them to like us, and we tell ourselves we just need more time to show them how great we are. So next time someone says how great they think you are or how much they love you BUT they just don't want anything serious, believe every word they say. Don't overanalyze it and try to figure out how they can love you but not want to be with you. And don't let your friends convince you that they are just afraid of commitment, and when they say they love you it's their subconscious crying out for help, and you need to fight for the both of you. No, don't do that. That is insanity. Just simply listen to what they're saying. When they tell you, believe them.

I know what you're thinking—but what if they say they love you? If you want to know why a fuckboy can say they love you and still not want to be with you, it's not because they are scared, it's because they are selfish. Maybe they do love you, but it's love from someone who is in a very selfish state of mind with a very limited amount to give to anyone else. And this is not how you want or need to be loved. We can all be selfish. Some of us more than others, but one could argue there are times to be selfish and there are times to be giving in our lives. The trick is finding the right balance.

Avoiding the wrong people is so hard, and the least we can do to protect ourselves is listen to the ones who are up front about it.

FIVE HALLMARKS OF THE PLAYER

The good news is that the five signs of fuckboys also apply to players, so you don't have to learn a whole different set of rules. There are just five additional qualities to look out for in order to determine if someone is a player.

1 They have a history of cheating.

This should be an obvious sign, but so many of us choose to ignore it because our egos tell us that we have to see for ourselves if a person can't be trusted, instead of just looking at their history—this is equally true if you are the person they're cheating with. As I said in the first part of this book, our egos want us to believe we're the special ones, the ones the cheaters finally treat with respect. As usual, our egos are wrong.

2 Lots of people warn you about them.

You can't be liked by everyone. People constantly tear down others for stupid, pointless reasons. As such, I am not saying that a little criticism about someone you're dating is reason enough to run, but players leave a trail of destruction behind them. There are typically several stories out there about a player's negative behavior if you're willing to hear them. If somebody tells you to be careful, or ask so-and-so about them, maybe don't ignore their advice.

 ### They constantly objectify women.

If you're dating a guy that is constantly talking about other women's bodies or criticizing them, there is a good chance this guy is a player (and a total piece of shit). This person does not respect women. They talk down to them; they dismiss them. If you ask this person to give their opinion on another hetero relationship, they will almost always take the man's side, no matter how problematic the situation.

 ### They gaslight you.

Gaslighting is a tactic people use in order to gain more power. It makes their victims question reality by insisting that the evidence they see doesn't add up to what they think. For example: The person you're dating is constantly at clubs and calls you at three in the morning to come over. When they do, they reek of perfume, have lipstick on their collar, and a hickey on their neck. When you ask them if they've been with other women that night, they accuse you of being crazy and paranoid. Their goal is to constantly keep you on the defense. That way, while you're busy justifying your sanity, they're free to add you to their list of conquests.

They love bomb you.

Love bombing is an attempt to influence a person by demonstrations of attention and affection. Essentially, they shower you with words and affirmations that feel equally premature and inconsistent. They will drop the "L" word on you seemingly out of nowhere—especially when they are losing control or power in the relationship. A major signal that someone might be love bombing you is that it's typically done while someone is trying to coerce you into something, like hooking up or not leaving them after they cheated on you. It's usually preceded by the word "but": "But, I love you, don't leave me" or "Come on, I love you." They want you to feel grateful for the love and affection and never question that they could be disingenuous. News flash—they don't really love you. They are players who have no problem teasing you with the thing you want in order to get what they want.

Again, people want to hear those words—it feels great—but if it seems early or fast or slightly on the defensive, there's nothing wrong with asking, "Why do you love me?" "Why do you feel the way you do?" "Oh, that's so nice of you to say it, but why do you have those feelings for me?" If someone can't articulate why they love you beyond, "I just do" or "You're cool" or "You're amazing," then it's probably not love. It might be infatuation. It might be a lie. Saying "I love you" should not be just some flippant feeling. It's not something that you say because it feels good in the moment. Maybe they even think they do love you—but don't assume they love you the way you expect to be loved. Do you have any idea what the concept of love means to them? There's a million different versions of what love means to people. Be careful putting so much weight on what someone says if you don't have a clear understanding of what they mean. I think a lot of us get caught up in those words and are afraid of questioning them, because they feel so good to hear.

I just want to add that you shouldn't read this book and then go start diagnosing the people you're dating or the people your friends are dating based off of what I'm telling you. If you think that you are being love bombed or gaslit on, or you think your friend is, maybe run that by an actual therapist, or reference book—not the internet and not me. Both of these terms are meant for serious things—gaslighting is a systematic, ongoing effort to truly try to alter someone's reality. It is not disagreeing about how to see a situation. It is not being so frustrated with your partner that you say things like, "I never said that!" That's maybe not gaslighting, that's a disagreement.

The bigger takeaway could be that you don't need to know these terms to set boundaries, to enforce boundaries, to think about why you're staying in a relationship that makes you feel bad more than you feel great. If you wake up in this relationship and you feel miserable, why are you choosing to stay in it? That's the more important thing.

BONUS: SPOTTING A CHEATER

Maybe you don't know this player, you have no friends in common, and you're wondering if you should date them. How do you know if they're a cheater? When I was twenty-eight, I got engaged to my then-girlfriend. Just after we got engaged, a lot of my friends said, "We've just got to tell you—she's cheating on you," but I just didn't want to hear it. I convinced myself of some alternate truth because my ego couldn't handle it. I wasn't prepared to think that anyone could cheat on me, let alone someone that I just proposed to. I was like, *I am engaged to this person, I need to trust her.* That's love—trusting someone, blah, blah, blah, blah, blah. I just didn't want to look at what was right in front of me, but it was all right there, and in retrospect, I saw plenty of the signs before my friends even told me. I always like to say that shavings make a pile—small things add up to something big.

Part of what is hard about being willing to acknowledge the pile of evidence is that our ego doesn't want to admit that we were played, that we were deceived for so long. I think that's why catfishing works, even when the cover stories seem like such outrageous lies. Once you get in deep enough that you can see that it is all a lie, it's too hard to face. So I just didn't look. But from that experience, I learned how to spot a cheater—these are (some of) the signs.

1. Are there gaps in their timeline? Can they really account for days or hours when you didn't see them? Do they randomly disappear and you don't know where they are?

2. If you ask them questions about certain things that should be easy to answer—where they were or who they were with, for example—do they get triggered or angry? Or are the answers they give you confusing?

3. Why do they have all these quote-unquote good friends or colleagues that call or text that you've never heard of before?

4. If they have friends of the opposite sex, but are reluctant for you to be friends with those friends. Or perhaps the same gender, if they're LGBTQIA. (If it's the friend that is trying to keep you at arm's length, it doesn't necessarily mean they're hooking up with your partner, but it definitely means that person isn't 100 percent onboard about respecting your relationship.)

5. At the end of the day, if it feels off, it probably is. Trust your gut. Someone once asked me, "How do you tell the difference between being paranoid and trusting your gut?" Being paranoid is creating new scenarios in your head and then responding to that, and trusting your gut is responding to something that your partner actually did.

If this is sounding familiar to you, I urge you to open your eyes to the situation. Your ego might be keeping you from seeing the signs—*I couldn't be cheated on, not me*—but by ignoring these warning signs, you're not saving face, you're just wasting your own time.

WHEN FUCKBOYS BECOME SITUATIONSHIPS

If you're not paying attention to the red flags, and you don't actively communicate or enforce your boundaries with a fuckboy or a player, you could end up in a long-term situationship.

What exactly is a situationship, anyway? (Beyond a new dating term that has become completely mainstream in just the past ten years.) Psychotherapist Jonathan Alpert—the author of a self-help book called *Be Fearless*—has described a situationship as "that space between a committed relationship and something more than a friendship." The *Today* show described it as "less than a relationship, but more than a casual encounter or booty call, a situationship refers to a romantic relationship that is, and remains, undefined."

There is something about those now-common descriptions that I don't like. They make a situationship sound so neutral. As if it is something that can randomly happen, and even worse, that it is now another completely valid and acceptable type of relationship status. To be honest, it sounds like how a fuckboy might describe a situationship—"Well, it is what it is."

I'll give you a more honest and helpful interpretation of a *situationship*: It is a romantic connection where one party is avoiding a relationship while the other party hopes that changes. My definition has a point of view, which is that a situationship is not something that is just randomly occurring, it's happening because people are making choices, and it's those choices that are creating the situationship.

Since I'm already picking a fight with *Today*'s definition, I also want to point out that I don't think it is accurate to say a situationship remains undefined. That implies that there has been no attempt by either party to define the romantic connection, as though situationships are just two people who are romantically involved, but haven't gotten around to chatting about taking the next step. While I'm sure that does happen, I'm willing to bet that most of you who consider yourselves to be in a situationship have very much attempted to try to define things. More specifically, you wanted to be in a relationship, only to have the other person provide some reason why they need to continue to define themselves as being single.

From this perspective, the situation is very much defined. It isn't the definition you wanted, and that's why it's a situationship, and not a relationship. Sorry, *Today*.

To be clear, this isn't me trying to one-up people who are almost certainly smarter than me. I am just making the point that a situationship isn't something to strive for, or even to accept. In a situationship, you are faced with accepting less than what you want with someone. You end up trying to compromise with yourself about what you are willing to give and accept. If you find yourself in a situationship, you should do whatever you can do to get out of it, because all you are doing is compromising the boundaries you wanted to set with a person you wanted to be in a relationship with.

Occasionally you might also find that you are in a relationship—you may call each other boyfriend or girlfriend, and in theory you are committed—but in practice it more closely resembles a situationship. If you find yourself constantly wanting more and always accepting less, whether it is more of their time or more emotional commitment or just to meet their friends, you might technically be dealing with a situationship. That's because there are plenty of people who love having the title of girlfriend or boyfriend, but hate the expectations that come with it. In other words, they have no interest in actually being a girlfriend or boyfriend.

Thinking about priorities is one way to evaluate whether both parties are on the same page and not just biding their time in a situationship until someone better comes along. You should be a top priority to the person you're in a real relationship with. You shouldn't be their only priority, but you shouldn't be their last priority after everything else, either—their family and their job and their friends and their hobbies.

Understanding where you are in someone else's list of priorities is key to determining if you're with someone who wants some of the benefits of a partner but doesn't really want a serious relationship or, more specifically, doesn't really want you to be their serious partner. Because there's a huge difference, and it's important to recognize the difference, which you can do by thinking hard about where you fall in the list of things they put first. Does the person you're with consistently put you first at least some of the time? If you realize you're almost never a top priority, it means setting a boundary and sticking to it—the boundary being that if they can't or won't make you a priority some of the time, then you walk away—because you shouldn't accept less than you want in a relationship.

That said, the easiest way for anyone to solve any kind of situationship is to ... drumroll ... COMMUNICATE! You communicate and tell that person, "I want to be with you. I'm falling for you. Hell, I have already fallen. I love you. I want so much more with you. I don't want to be just friends or the occasional hookup. I want to be a priority in your life."

As I've said, most of us choose not to do that out of fear of hearing the answer we don't want. Nevertheless, it's the most efficient way of identifying if there is a chance that this might change, while simultaneously starting the healing process. Once you communicate your vulnerability, it's like a cleanse that will get you to start feeling healthy again. It may not heal you as fast as you want, or in the manner that you want, but you will feel better. Communicating what you want—setting expectations and boundaries—and holding yourself accountable after you do it will get the person you are in a situationship with to either choose you, because losing you is something they would rather not do, or make it very clear that they're never going to choose you. I also think it's good to remember that if your situationship turns you down after you try to define things, they aren't really rejecting you, they are just rejecting what you want.

In case you still need some clarification, here's a breakdown of two of the most common types of situationships.

The Just-Got-Out-of-a-Relationship Situationship.

I had a guy call in on an episode of my podcast, a young man who was dating a woman who had been recently divorced when they started dating. It had been a fairly long marriage. And by the time he called in to the podcast, he had been dating her for almost a year, but it was really a situationship.

Situationships are very common. You know, you're hanging out with someone for a somewhat long period of time. There's some consistency there—you're hooking up on a regular basis. Once in a while you go out to dinner, you're kind of playing house every once in a while, but you're probably not talking every day. You're not meeting their parents or spending time with their friends. And one person always says, "I don't want a relationship right now." But they do like having someone who is there to spend the night with, to have consistent sex with, to go to movies with, to have dinner with. They like that if they get invited to a wedding, they have a date, and all those superficial benefits that come with having a girlfriend or boyfriend. A lot of people just like having that person around even if they're not the person.

With my caller, this woman would try to avoid any discussions of being exclusive, any talk of entering into a more serious relationship. She would even talk about how she was kind of seeing some other guy too. She had been divorced for a year and a half by that time, and yet still referenced the divorce as the reason she couldn't commit. In all honesty, someone fresh out of a marriage might not yet be ready for that next big relationship, but that's where being honest and setting expectations comes in. Instead, she kept wanting to hang out with him. She kept wanting to have sex with him, for him to be there when she wanted to see him. She would say things suggesting that she wasn't sure if she wanted to spend the rest of her life with him, because she'd already been married and that didn't work, et cetera, et cetera, et cetera. They would start to have sex more often, and then they would slow things down. Then they would start talking again, start sleeping with each other again—but nothing ever really changed.

Now reader, I ask you, having read the above, are you confused about what's going on here? No, you're not. It's clear that these two people are seeking different things from the relationship. It's clear that, to her, this caller was just an option.

And here is this guy on the other end of the line with me, confused. He liked her. He wanted to date her, to be with her. But at this point he was afraid of even asking for any sort of commitment again because he was afraid if he brought it up, he would lose the part of her he did have. He would rather have just some of her, he told me, if he couldn't have all of her. And so he didn't do anything.

Now, she wasn't a horrible person. She wasn't lying, she wasn't even being super deceitful. She probably did care about his feelings, but ultimately, she wanted to be a little bit selfish, to actively go out and date and have the freedom to hang out with anyone she wanted, but also, you know, have sex with him when she wanted that too.

In short, she was being a fuckboy, and fuckboys will usually bring up a reason they can't be in a relationship. Maybe that reason seems reasonable, at first, like a divorce. *This person just got a divorce,* you think to yourself, *of course they'd be cautious.* That seems totally fair. But, as I told him, how long is a divorce actually a reasonable reason not to be in a relationship with someone? A year? Two years? She's going to meet some other guy, and he's going to sweep her off her feet, and she's going to say, "I don't care that I only got divorced a year and a half ago."

As I said, she's not a bad person. What this was was two people being afraid of being more open with their feelings, because neither person wanted to lose what they had—even though the value they each saw in the relationship was different. When it comes to fuckboys, especially these long-term fuckboys, a lot of it comes down to our own choices. We're choosing not to set boundaries, or to ignore the ones we have set. A lot of times we will create these situationships—we do it when we know we want more, but we're willing to accept less, because we're afraid.

We want to date them. We want them to commit to us. We want to be with them, no one else. Maybe we've even hinted to the other person, maybe we've floated the idea or brought it up in the past—but even after the other person says no, or avoids the question, we're still there when they want to have sex. We'll keep hanging out.

And that's what my caller had been doing—he would put up with that painful situation, and convince himself it wasn't that bad. This woman kept saying to him, "I don't want a relationship right now," and she couldn't be more truthful. Except my caller kept hearing those words "right now," and telling himself that "right now" could change.

He didn't ask more questions that might end in an answer that he didn't want to hear—that "not right now" means never. He didn't want to push her for an answer not just because he was afraid of pushing her away, but also because he was afraid of the truth. And the truth is not that she didn't want a relationship right now, she just didn't want a relationship with him.

The Sour-Patch-Kid Situationship.

I like to call the worst level of situationship a Sour Patch Kid. This is a term I made up a few years back after I attended the birthday party of a woman I was dating at the time. It was a small party, and this was the first time I was meeting her family and circle of friends. I had previously met her sister and had developed a bit of a rapport with her. Being the introvert that I am, I set up camp next to her sister so I had someone to shoot the breeze with and not worry about randomly floating in the middle of the room with nothing but my neurotic thoughts to keep me company.

Anyway, as the sister got more comfortable with me, she began to talk to me about this guy she had been "hanging out with" for well over a year. It was a coworker, someone a few years younger than her. They had been hooking up, going on dates, and getting to know each other. She wanted to be with him but never really directly expressed that to him. She would suggest it in passing, sometimes float the idea as an option, passive-aggressively dropping little hints about wanting to take the next step. However, she never fully crossed the line of being vulnerable enough to say, "I want to be with you. I'm falling for you. Hell, I have already fallen. I love you. I don't want to be just friends. I want so much more with you." Or some version of that.

Confiding how she actually felt would mean having to hold him and herself accountable to follow through on the fact that she can't be just friends. But, of course, the alternative was torture. That is what she was doing—torturing herself by wanting so much more and accepting less. Hoping that he would one day want to give up his current lifestyle, a lifestyle that already included getting to sleep with her and go on dates with her essentially any time he felt like it. When he would feel vulnerable and lonely, he would reach out to her.

To justify all this energy she was investing, she would tell herself this was a sign that he needed her. That him needing her would be a reminder to him that she was worth committing to, and eventually that would click for him too. That is the dream, to connect with someone who chooses you. Loves you so much that they don't want an emotional or physical connection with anyone else. They are willing to make sacrifices and compromises for the person they love and the connection they want to grow. The good news is that it's possible. It happens every day. It can happen to everyone. The bad news is that the world is full of people we get immediate enjoyment from being around who we confuse for potential candidates for this type of love we are searching for. People who give us instant gratification to the max. Except the problem for us is that they are toxic, and when we have too much of them, they make us sick.

While I was talking to the sister, she was going into all the details of the relationship. Me being who I am, I was fascinated by her story and wanted to see if I could try to help solve her problem. Her biggest problem was that she didn't even know what her real problem was. She would talk about the slight age difference. The fact that they worked together. I don't totally remember all the details, but she probably said something about a past girlfriend who broke his heart or a parent who didn't connect with him as a child. She was looking at all these challenges as the reasons she wasn't getting what she wanted, and while all of the aforementioned challenges are certainly real and valid obstacles that couples face all the time, none of them have stopped a couple from being together if that is something they both want. Her main problem was that he didn't want to commit to her, full stop. Her secondary problem was that she was convinced that wasn't true.

I wanted to figure out a way to explain to her how I was understanding her logic. I wanted to repeat it back to her how I was hearing it, and have it seem as obvious to her as it did to me that her problem was him. I thought of one of my favorite candies. My toxic friend, the Sour Patch Kid. I fucking love this candy. My mouth literally salivated just now as I typed its name and thought about the wonderfully sour and sweet candy. They are so good, insanely good. They are also toxic as shit. The enjoyment I get out of eating a whole bag is eventually met with feeling kind of sick. Potential stomachaches, bloating, fatigue, and a slew of subtle discomfort. Let me just list for you the ingredients of Sour Patch Kids. Sugar, inverted sugar, corn syrup, modified corn starch, tartaric acid, citric acid, natural and artificial flavor, yellow 6, red 40, yellow 5, blue 1. The healthiest ingredient in that pile of trash is sugar. Sugar! Which creates inflammation in our bodies, and inflammation is essentially the main cause for every health problem that we have. So yeah . . . pretty bad.

To be honest, the existence of sugar alone makes me believe in a higher power. It's so crazy to me that something so enjoyable can be equally as toxic. If God exists, there is no way He doesn't have a sense of humor. Creating something so delicious and addictive only to essentially make it a slow-working poison for no real reason other than His own amusement—just think about that. If God doesn't exist, I want a scientist to break down for me why in the course of evolution it was decided that sugar was going to be both unbelievably good and horrifyingly bad for us, because there has to be a reason.

So, anyway, sugar is bad. No conscious adult is under the illusion that sugar is good for us. Yes, we all consume it, but we do so with the understanding that there are some risks. We know we can't survive on a diet that primarily consists of sugar. If we take in too many toxic ingredients and not enough healthy nutrients, we get sick. Knowing there is risk, most of us try to limit our sugar indulgence. Those who have a harder time having that willpower still understand that if they want change, self-discipline is a good place to start. The good news is, it's pretty easy to spot sugar: Just read the label. The government legally requires that companies have to let us know approximately how much sugar we're consuming when we eat their products.

Unfortunately, humans don't have clear ingredient labels. With people, it's harder to identify who has qualities that are toxic and harmful to us and who has qualities that will nurture us. Usually we have to first take a bite to determine what category someone falls into. We try them out and pay attention to how we feel afterward. Is there a relatively consistent state of feeling good, or is it extreme highs and lows of enjoyment and discomfort? If it's more the latter, then it's a good bet that they are a Sour Patch Kid and you need to stop trying to enjoy them or you'll get sicker and sicker.

So, what makes someone a Sour Patch Kid? Sour Patch Kids are usually created in one of two ways. The first is trauma from their past. The second and most common way is just that they have really terrible communication skills and don't respect boundaries. In either scenario, this is not someone who has promise as a potential partner. Sour-Patch-Kid situations are usually less common as we get older and are exposed to different life experiences: For most of us, this causes us to become better communicators.

But let's say your Sour Patch Kid is dealing with past trauma. If you haven't heard of attachment styles you should look into them, but, essentially, experiences from our pasts, especially trauma from our childhood, can impact how we connect with people and, more importantly, how we disconnect. By and large, even if we have flaws, we are able to connect with people, and even forge deep and meaningful bonds. For some, however, their trauma stops them from connecting with anyone at all. The most extreme examples would be someone with a narcissistic personality disorder—though the majority of people aren't true narcissists, they just have some serious shit to work through. Working through that serious shit requires time and help that cannot come from a romantic partner. Only a therapist can help someone through whatever attachment disorder they might have, and most of you reading this aren't therapists, and neither am I. (This is true whenever I discuss serious psychological issues in this book.)

We are just going to have to accept that until that therapy happens, this person will be as toxic to us as Sour Patch Kids are. They are just going to continue to make us sick, sad, and leave us feeling unhealthy. For a Sour Patch Kid of this type to magically turn into broccoli without a crazy amount of work is unlikely—and your time is too valuable to simply wait for a miracle.

Bottom line with any Sour Patch Kid is that as much as this person is really enjoyable at first, if you want to feel healthy, you're going to have to find the willpower and strength to be honest, and likely start looking for people that will be able to nourish your heart.

In case you were wondering, the sister eventually was able to stop indulging in the thing that was making her sick. It didn't happen overnight. Once she listened to my Sour-Patch-Kid theory, she finally started to accept that her problem was him, but that still doesn't always make it easy for us to suddenly give up our favorite candy. I hate how eating too many Sour Patch Kids makes me feel, but goddamn it, once in a while I say, "Fuck it." It took her some time too. And sure, the cravings got intense sometimes, but once she started feeling better it got easier to say no because the relief of feeling consistently good started to have a stronger pull on her than the instant gratification of that candy binge.

CAN YOU TRANSFORM A SITUATIONSHIP INTO A RELATIONSHIP?

I think it's very important to start this section off by reminding you that most situationships won't end up as relationships. Most of them end as soon as someone starts enforcing boundaries. However—very rarely—you might be in a situationship with someone who is just a little slow to realize you're worth the investment, and who just needs a little push, a little inspiration, to get out of their own way. How do you know if that's your situationship? The first step is to stop making the two major mistakes people in long-term situationships usually make.

Mistake number one: Faking it till you make it.

There are many points in life where I am a big believer in faking it till you make it—except when it comes to situationships, when it's a major mistake. Many people who want a situationship to move to a real relationship will often try to create as many moments as they can that feel like a real relationship—with the hope that the other person will one day realize how great things are and commit. (I can't tell you how many questions I get that say something like, "They say they can't be in a relationship with me, but they act like they do all the time." Usually they aren't acting like they are in a relationship with you, they just don't mind having dinner with you on a regular basis or going shopping with you, because who wants to do those things alone?)

The truth is, you acting like you're in a relationship when you're in a situationship only decreases the chances of things changing. All you're doing is showing them how much you are willing to do for them without them meeting any of your relationship expectations. I bet that if you called them out for doing what you deem "real relationship" stuff, they would just offer to stop doing it—and remind you that they said they can't be in a relationship right now.

Mistake number two: Taking yourself off the market.

For whatever reason, it's very common for the person on the hopeful side of the situationship to just stop dating anyone else, even though the other person has made it clear that they won't be exclusive with them. I have been that person in the past, and I have made this same mistake. It makes no sense that so many of us who wanted more from someone decided to make it clear to that someone that we are just going to accept less. I suppose the thought process is, *We're letting them know how serious we are, and how much they mean to us.*

Except that never works. It doesn't work because all you are really saying is, "Take your time, I'm not going anywhere. Go look for something better, and I'll put myself on hold, just in case you change your mind." But remember that a situationship is not a relationship, and if it's not a relationship, well, then you are single. I repeat, you are single!!! And if you're single, you should at least give the appearance of still being available to meet other people.

On the other hand, some of you in situationships might still date other people, but maybe you're actively trying to keep it from the person you are in your situationship with—out of fear that they will get upset and leave. This is just not smart, for a couple of reasons. One, you're wasting the opportunity to casually let them find out you're highly desired by many other people, and two, you're already being dishonest with someone you're hoping to grow a real relationship with.

So no more faking it till you make it, and go ahead and put yourself back on the dating market, or be honest that you're still dating. Now, you can use my step-by-step situationship hack to turn your situationship into a relationship—and again, this only works if you're in a situation with someone who just needs a little push to get out of their own way.

Before I give you this tutorial, let's talk about the idea of playing games. No matter what I say, some of you are going to read what follows and think, *Ugh, that sounds like playing games. I don't play games.* If I am doing my job with this book, then hopefully I already sound like someone who doesn't promote playing games with dating, but the reality is we all do, from time to time—with ourselves. Games are played when you lie or avoid the truth about your intentions. So we all play games with ourselves, because we all have egos that are constantly searching for validation or avoiding facing truths.

Think about all those little lies we like to tell ourselves in situationships—when we agree to just one more hookup, when we tell ourselves we do this because we just want the sex, or that we won't be sad or upset when they don't call the next day—those are the games we play with ourselves.

As I write this, I am currently debating with my editor what the title of this book should be, and you could make a strong case that it should be something like, *The Games We Shouldn't Play With Ourselves.* So yeah, I'm not promoting playing games. But if we are keeping it real, you don't end up in a situationship without playing games with yourself, and trying to convince yourself that you're okay with constantly accepting less. So, what I'm about to tell you could be called gamesmanship, but really, all you're going to do is be honest with the person you're in a situationship with.

So here we go: If you find yourself in a situationship and want to see if you can transition it to a relationship, follow these steps:

1. Make sure you have first clearly attempted to communicate and define the relationship with the person you are in a situationship with (see page 113).
2. If they say they don't want a relationship, and you have decided to still spend time with them or try to change their mind, do so only with the mindset and the appearance that you are still fully single. Make sure you're still on the apps and that your DMs are open and that the world sees you as single. I'm not suggesting you desperately try to set up multiple dates, I am simply saying you must go forward knowing that you're still available.
3. At some point, go on some dates with other people. Even if all you can think about is how much you wish it was a date with your situationship, challenge yourself to get out there from time to time. I don't care if it's just a cup of coffee, a Zoom date, or a walk, just do it. First, the more you go on these dates, the more you increase the chances of meeting someone else you like. And second, at some point, your situationship will reach out and ask you what you're up to when you are about to go on a date. When that happens, the next steps are very important.

4. Do not for any reason whatsoever cancel a date to hang with your situationship! I don't care what they ask you to do, or how unexcited you are for the date. DO NOT CANCEL!

5. If your situationship asks what you're doing when you're about to go on a date, Tell them! "I am getting ready for a date." That's all you say. You don't give them any more information. You want them wondering. You want them surprised at how worried they are getting. They will likely try to act unbothered and pretend that they don't care. They might say, "Oh yeah, that's exciting." Then they will probably ask you who the date is with. Don't respond. First off, it's none of their business. Second, you're busy getting ready for your date. Or they may follow up with a "?" by text, or something like that. Eventually you can reply with, "Sorry, I'm just in a rush." Again, you want them stewing. If they call, don't answer.

6. Your situationship may keep digging for who the date is with, and will probably even accuse you of avoiding the question, or something to that effect. Then you can reply back with their first name only. His name is Josh. Her name is Shasha. This will make it feel more real to them. Don't offer any more information. If they dig for it, wait some more, and then just write back something like, "Sorry, running out the door. Can we talk tomorrow?" No matter what, do not reply to them for the rest of the night—after all, you're on a date, and you should be focused on Josh or Shasha.

7. Let them follow up with you, not vice versa. Do not at any point apologize. Don't offer any information about the date, regardless of how the date goes. You don't need to oversell it, and certainly don't let them know if you didn't enjoy yourself. Again, it's none of their business.

8. If they show any frustrations with your honesty, do not act defensive! You should simply say you're confused. You're confused because you have already made it clear you want them, but they don't want you. They may try to make you feel bad, or say why they are justified in being frustrated. You just keep calm, and remind them that you're both single, and if they're interested in changing that to let them know.

There you go. That is all you have to do. If this doesn't work, remember it was never going to—and you're already many steps closer to finding someone who will give you what you want and what you deserve.

Now, some of you might also be thinking, *Nick! There's no way this will work. If I did all that, they would be turned off and everything would be ruined.* To which I would say, you didn't ruin anything. You just got an answer you have been trying to avoid. If your situationship is turned off by this, or doesn't seem to care, then all you ruined was the ability for one person to stroke their ego by getting someone to sit on the sidelines and wait for them. You didn't ruin your chances with anyone who was ever going to commit to you in the way that you wanted them to.

When dealing with situationships, I also want you to think about this one final thing. I am sure you have all seen the movie or read the book *He's Just Not That Into You.* I have been told a lot of what I talk about has a similar feeling. The big takeaway from that book was realizing that you're not the exception to the rule—that everyone out there wants to believe they are the one for the person they want to be with, but in reality, they are not.

I think there is a lot of truth to that, but I don't think that idea is all that helpful when you're excited about someone. I think that the more important thing is to be honest when you're trying to be the exception to the rule. There is nothing wrong with taking risks and being vulnerable in a situation that may not work out the way you hope. Just don't lie to yourself about what you're trying to do. Be honest about what you want, and be realistic about the risks and the effort trying to get it will require.

QUESTIONS WITH NICK

Q:

Met a guy and we click on lots of levels but especially sexually. Should I worry he's only in it for that?

A:

Tell him how you feel . . . literally zero downside. If that spooks him, he didn't want to date you anyway. If you're worried about spooking him, then maybe you're okay with just hooking up with him and you're judging yourself. If you're worried he will lie to you and ghost you anyway . . . tell him after you express your desire to date that if he ghosts you, you will absolutely go crazy and lose your shit on him . . . but other than that, you're chill AF. He'll be honest then.

Q:

How to politely tell a guy who's really into you not to get his hopes up too much.

A:

When you tell someone not to get their hopes up, you're implying there is hope. So, if you really don't think there is a chance, then tell them there is no chance. Don't keep hanging out with him when you're bored.

QUESTIONS WITH NICK

Q:

Is it okay to go to a holiday party with a guy you just met? Like known for two days only?

A:

Sure it's okay, but have low expectations and proceed with caution. Also . . . tell your friends where you are going, in case he murders you.

Q:

Slept with a random guy from the bar. Now he wants to take me out. Just nice or wants to?

A:

Guys aren't that nice. He must want to get to know you.

Q:

I want a relationship but he wants a hookup . . . what do I do?

A:

Commit to what you want him to commit to. Let him know your desire for a relationship is a bigger priority than his.

QUESTIONS WITH NICK

Q:

How do you attract decent guys and fewer jerks?

A:

Did you know that our brains require stimulation? As a result our brains prefer pain to boredom. When it comes to dating, we get lonely, impatient, and bored. So, we say yes to things that give us stimulation. Even when it's only pain. If you keep saying yes to boredom, good chance you won't be available when something good comes along.

Q:

There is this guy who wants to date me but he's a player. Should I just be friends or risk it?

A:

Whatever you decide, just know you won't change him. That person doesn't exist.

Q:

He said he wanted a relationship when we first met. We hook up all the time, but he still hasn't committed. It's been six months. What gives?

A:

A well-intentioned fuckboy is still a fuckboy.

QUESTIONS WITH NICK

Q:

Why do men tell women things just because women want to hear it?

A:

Because they want short-term gratification.

Q:

Thoughts on a thirty-year-old man who ghosted me but wanted my babies the day before, lol.

A:

Believe the actions, not the words.

Q:

This boy I've been seeing keeps disappearing and coming back. What the actual fuck is going on?

A:

Possibilities:
A magician
Transporting X-Men
A wizard
A ghost
Just an immature BOY

QUESTIONS WITH NICK

Q:

Guy wants hookups only. Told him it's best if we are only friends. He still messages me. Why?

A:

He's hoping you get bored and change your mind.

Q:

Thoughts on reaching out to a guy who's been ghosting me for the last two weeks?

A:

If he wanted to be found, he wouldn't disappear.

Q:

I slept with this guy after knowing him two days. He was way into me before and now he's not.

A:

He was very into wondering what it was like to have sex with you. Now he knows.

QUESTIONS WITH NICK

Q:

How to get over a guy that you know isn't good for you but still like anyway?

A:

I made this chart to help put things in perspective:

	Person I know isn't right for me but can't get over	Sour patch kids
I get excited just thinking about them	x	x
hard to have in moderation	x	x
I know they are bad for me	x	x
when I have too much of them, I end up not feeling well	x	x
ignore how bad they made me feel last time. Have again	x	x
Try to give them up..but when I get bored/hungry and they are around I tend to give in	x	x
Will never be able to give me the nourishment that I need to feel good	x	x

When you accept you can't live off Sour Patch Kids, you will move on.

Q:

Sex with exes . . . ?

A:

This is the exact same as selecting a diet of only Sour Patch Kids as the solution to feeling your physical best. Amazing in the moment . . . followed by immediate regret and feeling rotten on the inside.

QUESTIONS WITH NICK

Q:

He stopped texting me after texting every day, so I deleted him and now I regret it.

A:

You only regret it because it didn't make him chase you. Now you're second guessing yourself wondering if a different action would have worked. You did the right thing even if you didn't get the outcome you wanted.

Q:

Do guys ever get out of a fuckboy phase?

A:

Yes, but it never feels like it because fuckboys rarely, if ever, change for the people they are being fuckboys to. They change for people they want to make a priority, not for people who allow themselves to be options.

Q:

Why do fuckboys always come back when you stop putting in the effort and match their energy?

A:

Fuckboys don't respond to love and affection. They respond to challenges.

QUESTIONS WITH NICK

Q:

Why do guys only want to have sex with me, then dip when it seems like a relationship might happen?

A:

Because you're having sex with guys who are not looking for a relationship. If you want to avoid this you need to be up front with expectations about sex and desire for a relationships before having sex with them. This won't completely solve your problem because some people lie, but it will filter out a lot of bad options. Trust your gut, it usually doesn't fail.

Q:

Guy says he doesn't want a girlfriend but does all the boyfriend things. What does he really want?

A:

To have consistency with you all while having the freedom to explore other options. Also, the freedom to have sex with other women when the opportunity comes.

Q:

Is it bad when a guy tells you to remind him you have plans to hang out?

A:

It is if you want to be a priority.

QUESTIONS WITH NICK

Q:

How to find guys on dating apps that aren't on there just for sex?

A:

You've always had to dig through dirt to find gold.

Q:

Give a guy a chance to change even if you know he won't?

A:

How long would you wait for the power to teleport before you just book a flight?

Q:

Why am I hung up on someone I never actually dated?

A:

Because you have a version of them in your head. What you don't know about them you fill in with your imagination, giving them all the best attributes, you desire. Stop fantasizing. Start living.

Q:

Says he really likes me and what I bring to the table. Says he's trying but isn't ready. Help!

A:

You are an option he is considering. The only thing he is trying is trying you out.

CHAPTER 3

MAKING THE FIRST MOVE

WHO SHOULD MAKE THE FIRST MOVE?

First, I just want to remind you that I am not a pickup artist. This chapter is not about how to convince someone to like you, or tricking someone into liking you—this book is just some honest, basic dos and don'ts for meeting someone for the first time, asking out someone you consider a friend, or reaching out to them online. Second, it helps to remember that everyone can get nervous. Even people you find attractive. Even very attractive people. Consider the fact that the more traditionally attractive someone is, the more likely it is they have been hit on. The more someone gets hits on, often the more sensitive they are to rejection—the bigger the ego, the harder the fall. More often than not, very attractive people get very nervous when it comes to making the first move. This logic is more applicable when it comes to hitting on someone in person, but the point is still valid: You can't assume that just because you think a person is very attractive, they will automatically have the confidence to approach you first if they are interested in you.

Of all the questions that come up when it comes to talking about who should make the first move, man versus woman is still a very common way that this is framed. Traditional dating rules suggest that it's the man's role to make the first move. The common stereotype used to be that men prefer to pursue, while women prefer to be pursued. I haven't done any scientific studies regarding how common this stereotype still is in the modern dating world, but from what I have heard from talking to so many people about dating, it persists.

There are certainly many women willing to make a move of some kind on a man they have interest in, but I've talked to some women who still have an extremely rigid personal rule regarding this topic, and refuse to ever make the first move, often saying that the action says something about the man, or themselves, or the potential for the relationship to succeed. It doesn't—my own girlfriend made the first move with me. The only thing having a rule about never making the first move says is that the person with the rule probably confuses things that should be pet peeves with things that are non-negotiables.

Also, that they are probably difficult or particular or picky. If there are any women who are afraid to approach men because of what they think men will think, well, let me set you straight: Men don't care if women make the first move. And if they do, let that be a red flag that you most likely encountered a man with a lot of toxic male energy. If a man feels emasculated from being approached by a woman, it's a good bet he certainly has other problems as well.

The end result of having a rule about who makes the first move, or not making a first move because you're scared to, is that you limit your options. The more people you meet, encounter, and talk to, the more chances you will have to meet the person you are looking for. So, if there is a person you are interested in and you want to strike up a conversation, shoot your shot—because you never know when that opening might close.

APPROACHING SOMEONE IN PUBLIC

With the explosion of social media and dating apps, hitting on someone has never been easier, in part because it's never been so easy to avoid feeling rejected. When we slide into someone's DMs or send a message on a dating app it's pretty easy for the recipient to just not respond, and it's even easier to tell ourselves that the person who didn't respond to us didn't even see our message. Easy outs on both sides.

It's not that way at all if you find the courage to approach a stranger in public. With all the unknowns, odds are we will end up disappointed if we approach someone in public. They could not be single, you could not be their type, they could not be in the mood to talk to a stranger, they could be in the midst of a personal crisis . . . the list goes on. If you think I'm trying to scare you from ever hitting on a stranger in public again, I'm not. I absolutely think it has its place, and I personally think the world would be better for it if it happened more often, but so many of us have the wrong mindset.

And many people feel the same way—I hear it all the time—"How do I meet people other than on the dating apps? Other than getting really good at walking up to strangers and dealing with a lot of rejection?"

It's hard to put yourself out there and let someone know you're interested in getting to know them, only to immediately find out they are not interested in getting to know you. That's real vulnerability, and it's not easy on our egos to be rejected. (This is sadly extra true with some men, who can quickly turn mean to women who reject them.) But when you put a stranger on the spot like that, there is a good chance they are going to be guarded. Especially if it's a woman.

(To the hetero men reading this book, the fact that you're reading this suggests you are one of the good ones. Regardless, if you take the time to sit down and talk to a female friend or sister and ask them if they have ever had an experience with a man that made them feel uncomfortable or unsafe during this kind of interaction, 100 percent of them will have some kind of story that would justify why, when they are approached by a man they don't know, they will have their guard up—at least a little.)

So how do we approach people in public while still protecting our vulnerability and theirs? The answer is to change your narrative and your perspective. The mistake people make is thinking they deserve some reward for having the guts to be vulnerable. That expectation usually comes in the form of some sort of validation from the person being approached, and when that validation doesn't happen, things can get toxic fast.

Instead, approach a stranger with gratitude on your mind. As I said in the introduction (page 22), I have come to think of gratitude as the only feeling that can't become toxic—when you're really expecting nothing in return. When you pay someone a compliment expecting only gratitude, everyone has the chance to walk away happy. Everyone loves a sincere compliment that doesn't come with strings attached. So instead of walking up to someone, commenting on their looks, and immediately asking them out, maybe try just quickly introducing yourself and giving them a non-sexual compliment.

This idea came to me when I started seeing a lot TikToks featuring women and men talking about their pet peeves when it came to being hit on in public. One woman was like, "Hey guys, can you just stop walking up to women?" She was saying that she never wants a guy to approach her in public. And then I was seeing men saying in response, "Listen, women, we're not ever hitting on you anymore, because we don't want to be called creepy." And then other women jumped in with the opposite position, saying, "Please come talk to us, because we want to meet someone."

I'm sitting here thinking, *Well, that's not sustainable. How can we get past this?* In this period of time when we're trying to be more self-aware and we're trying to identify bad behaviors with dating and relationships and men and women, et cetera, et cetera—how can we still connect? So I spent some time thinking about how we can approach each other out in public and have it be a positive experience for both parties. I decided to take the gratitude approach. What if you just say something nice to someone and compliment them in a way anyone can appreciate and respond to—not anything about their looks or their body, but maybe just say, "Hey, thanks for making my day with that kind smile."

"Hi, I'm Nick, I just wanted to say running into you made my day. I hope you enjoy the rest of yours" has a much better chance of not ending with anyone feeling hurt than saying, "Hi, I just wanted to say you're beautiful. I'd love to take you to dinner."

The more you can make the first words out of your mouth feel like a compliment and not a request, the more likely you can both leave that interaction feeling positive, even if the interest isn't mutual.

And if the other person completely blows you off, you can think to yourself, *All I was trying to do is make someone's day.* You don't have to feel rejected, you can change your narrative. It might be kind of a corny idea, but I think the more you can put yourself in that head space, the less discouraged you will feel.

If you're going to walk up to a stranger and say anything to them, you have so little information about that person, you have to be prepared for anything. And rejection sucks. After we work up all this energy and courage to go hit on someone, we often subconsciously think that the other person owes us something, even if it's just politeness, even if it's just their consideration. And the truth is they don't owe us anything. If you instead focus on feeling grateful that you got to say something nice to someone, a non-offensive and nice thing you could say to literally anyone, you can leave the interaction feeling better about yourself no matter what. Since you're not expecting anything back and you focused on paying them a compliment, you can find solace in the fact that while they might not be interested or available you probably just made their day.

And trust me, if that person is interested in you, I'm pretty sure they'll make it clear that they don't mind you approaching them. They won't be in a rush to leave the interaction, and they won't ignore you. They might stop and say, "What's your name?" They might smile and pause. If you really are grateful for the opportunity to make someone else feel good, it does help put things in perspective and feel less scary. And once in a while, if it's the right person, it might lead to something more.

There are some people, a small percentage of people, who have the gift of being incredibly charming all the time . . . and then there's the rest of us. I am not a pickup artist going around with a list of the top ten ways to flirt with someone, but I think a lot of it is just showing an interest in someone. Making eye contact, asking questions, and asking follow-up questions—that's all you really need to do. In the right context, those simple and seemingly obvious things are going to feel like flirting. They are flirting! Because the other person is now thinking, *Wow, you're interested in me.*

Years ago, I was at a party and I saw this beautiful woman across the room playing party games. She turned around and started asking me questions—and then she was like, "Do you want to play with us?" We must have both been in our late twenties, or early thirties, and at that moment, it felt no different than us meeting at a high school party. She's like, "Hey, how's it going? Where are you from? Do you want to join us?" And she just kept asking more things about me.

She wasn't doing anything crazy to let me know she was interested, you know—she was just asking questions. She was giving me an invitation to keep talking to her. She focused her energy on me, and I think that's really all you need to do. If you are showing interest in someone and you're not afraid of a little bit of rejection, I think that's it. The more afraid you are of disappointment, the more nervous you'll get, and the more awkward it will be. And no one's hurt anyone's feelings by being polite and asking them a simple question, or extending a compliment that's not based on physical appearance.

That may not help you pick up a stranger in any situation, but there are other books out there for that.

SLIDING INTO SOMEONE'S DMs

Successfully sliding into someone's DMs has more to do with knowing the limitations and managing expectations. With social media connecting everyone, we have incredible access to virtually anyone in the world. Before social media, you had to hope for a chance encounter with a stranger at the grocery store to introduce yourself. Now you just have to look a crush up on Facebook or Instagram or whatever app and send them a note. We have incredible access with very little real information about what makes someone tick. Along with this access comes a lot of noise, competition, and skepticism. We must remain cautiously optimistic.

Social media is a tool, and the best way to use any tool is for its intended purpose. Tools also have limitations. The better we understand those limitations, the more effectively the tool can be used to meet our needs. Facebook and Instagram are the best platforms for direct messaging people that we may have a romantic interest in. These are visual platforms. When you connect with someone on a visual platform, they are going to want to see what you look like. It's possible to learn other things about someone based on what they share on their social, but it still only provides some of the story. And the truth is, attraction is important.

So now we understand that when we are sliding into someone's DMs we are using social media as a tool to get the job done—the job being introducing ourselves to someone for the first time. I can use a screwdriver to hammer in a nail, but I would much rather use a hammer to get the job done. So how do we use this hammer correctly? Well, there is no perfect way to use social media to meet someone. There are too many variables and too many unknowns in a DM slide, so there can be no perfect way. But there are, however, a few simple dos and don'ts that will allow us to use this tool most effectively.

1 Make sure your profile is public.

If you're going to operate in an environment where people expect to be able to use their eyes, then you better make sure people can see what you look like and who you are. You're introducing yourself for the first time, and the other person is going to want to gauge their physical attraction to you more than anything else because that's the information they can trust the most on a social media platform.

It amazes me how many people will slide into someone's DMs with their profile on private and just send some kind of note. I mean, how witty do you think you are that you can write something and get a response without the other person having the slightest clue what you look like? Most of you are just saying "Hi" anyway. And even for those of you who make some attempt at a clever come-on, you're likely no Casanova either. Don't think for a second that your tiny little thumbnail on your profile is getting the job done. If for some reason you can't make your account public because there's certain aspects of your private life you don't think your job would appreciate, then you better be sending a pic or two in that DM. Which, to be honest, is going to feel fishy. So really, if you don't feel comfortable having a public profile, then sliding into someone's DMs really might not be for you. People want as much information as they can get to let them know it's safe and worth their time to respond. Make it easy for them and let them see you.

My current girlfriend, Natalie, and I met when she slid into my DMs. At the risk of sounding superficial, I found Natalie to be stunningly beautiful, and so that piqued my curiosity immediately. But if her Instagram had been private, I would've looked at her tiny little profile picture and thought, *This woman seems like she might be really attractive, but I can't tell because it's a super-small picture, and since I can't see her feed, I can't even tell if she's real*, so I would've definitely ignored it.

2 Make sure your profile includes pictures of you.

Perhaps you have an Instagram that really isn't about you—it's about your dog and your woodworking hobby. That's totally great. But then, no one's going to know what you look like, so maybe don't slide into any DMs when you have like just a bunch of pugs and bespoke wind chimes as your whole Instagram.

Let's say you don't include pictures of yourself because you have some (very likely unfounded) insecurities about the way you look. Well, if you want to have a relationship, and you want to meet someone, at some point you're going to have to put yourself out there and risk disappointment. Whether it's a dating app or Instagram slideshow or meeting a stranger at a party or a bar or a library, you're going to have to show your face at some point, and yeah, you might get rejected. I'll never be Chris Hemsworth, but I can take care of myself mentally and health-wise, and I can ask my friends what looks good on me style-wise. You can also talk to your friend who is really good at social media, and also have them take a couple of nice pictures of you. And you should remember that everyone is attracted to different things, and someone not being attracted to you is not a judgment of your worth.

3 Never assume anything about the person in your first message.

No one likes to be told who they are or how predictable they are, especially from strangers or people they barely know. So, make sure not to lead with things like, "I think we would be good together" or "I bet we would have a lot of fun." It's always better to make people feel like you're curious about them, that you want to know more. They want to know that you find them interesting and intriguing. It's easy to want to disagree with someone who is making an assumption about who we are. When you say, "I think we would hit it off," sometimes it can make the other person think, *Well, I don't think we will.*

4 Open with a question.

Sometimes people don't write back because they aren't sure how to respond. Simple questions are easy to answer, and we love sharing our answers with anyone who will listen. Since all we really want when we DM someone is for them to write back, make it super easy for them with a really simple question—"What coffee shop is that?" "Where is that hiking trail?" "What's your favorite pizza place?" Like I said, either on or off Instagram people will mainly be focused on if they think you're cute or not, so just dangle a carrot with a tasty little question and hope they bite. This is also a low-stakes way for them to engage in conversation with you without feeling that they're committing to anything.

5 Use the information the platform provides you.

The most efficient way to initiate a conversation is to ask a specific question based on the information provided on the platform you're using. Find a picture they posted and ask a simple question about something in the picture. It's a really easy way to make it about them. I also recommend trying to be as unique as possible. The good news is that it doesn't take all that much to stand out when most people don't make the effort to be different. So don't ask a question about their looks. The less serious, the better. "I was wondering if that coffee pot comes in red?" I think if you're hitting on the right people, they will know you're not really interested in the coffee machine and that you're just being playful. If they are interested, they will respond. If they are not, they won't, and you move on.

 Never tease, criticize, or critique.

You aren't in eighth grade anymore. People have too many options and too much access to everyone else to waste their time with someone who opens by being a dick.

7 **Don't try to make a joke or be poetic, either.**

If you really want to try to impress someone with your sense of humor or personality, I wouldn't choose social media as the way to do it. So much of humor is nonverbal communication—think about comedians. Even with the best comedians, it's not just what they say, it's how they say it—their body language, their tone, all of it. Most of us are not comedians—and when you're just reaching out to someone cold turkey, jokes can misfire. Especially when you know very little about them. In the beginning, keep it simple. They know very little about you and you just don't know how they're going to read your tone. I'm not saying never tell a joke, but you better be sure it's pretty clear that it's a joke, and also that it's really funny to almost everyone.

And even if you're a real Robert Frost, you still don't get to write a poem on Instagram and impress a bunch of people. If Natalie, who I now know is super intelligent, was in fact a poet laureate and came up with an ode to send in her DM, I would have still been, "That's kind of weird for this woman to write me a really eloquent poem."

When you DM someone, there is always the fear that maybe they won't see it or that they forgot. These are two real possibilities. With that in mind, you are allowed one follow-up without a response before you start coming off as too aggressive or creepy. Your follow-up should have something to do with the simple, silly question that you already asked. You don't have to worry about it not making any sense because your original message will be sitting there for them to refer to. All you're doing is moving your message back to the top in the off chance they're more willing to respond. If you asked them if that coffee maker comes in red, then maybe your second message is "Bad news, found out they're sold out of red coffee machines. I would love to grab a drink with you sometime." DO NOT send a follow-up lecturing them on not responding to you. Do not give them any confirmation that they were smart to not reply. There is no reason to be embarrassed. Someone you know nothing about, and who knows nothing about you, didn't reply. Don't let the only information they learn about you be that you get mean when you don't get what you want.

If you remember nothing else, remember this: Keep it simple, ask questions, and don't get discouraged if they do not respond. There are plenty of people out there whose DMs (and hearts) are open.

ZOOM IS YOUR FRIEND

Whether it's talking in the dating apps or sliding into someone's DMs, people are spending way too much time having conversations with total strangers via text message–type communication. I think that's just a giant waste of time, especially when COVID showed us that there are clearly tools and resources that we can use to help us filter through an overabundance of choices in the dating world.

It's kind of funny thinking about it now, but when I was going through my first breakup—one of many breakups with my first girlfriend—dating apps and social media didn't exist, and dating websites still carried the stigma of "desperation." You also really couldn't simply look anyone up and ascertain their relationship status by taking stock of their social media.

At that time I had a legit fear: *How am I going to find love again?* I thought about all of the serendipitous moments, how lucky I was to meet that first person. And I remember having this very specific thought that it was just so hard to know who was available, who was single. I wasn't going around hitting on a bunch of women at bars, but I had anxiety, and I was nervous. That's when they used to have singles mixers or singles nights at bars. I'm sure events like that still exist to some degree, but it's less of a thing. You know, on Valentine's Day they'd have singles mixers—it'd be, "Let's just get the single people together, you know, so everybody knows everyone else there is single."

Fifteen years ago, we were complaining that there were no options, or that we didn't know how to find anyone. Now people still have those same complaints about dating apps—there are no options, or they can't find anyone. But in reality, it's more paralysis of choice. You can go on what feels like an endless number of dating apps and social media platforms at any given time. Any night, in any city, you can go on a dating app and have a date set up for later that night. It might not be with your favorite person. It might take a few swipes. It might not be super exciting, but anyone can do that in this day and age, if they want to. And that gives us an abundance of choice, an abundance of options.

What that really means is that we need to get better at filtering down our options. The algorithms do some of the work for us, but we still have to do the rest of it. What can you really learn from texting four total strangers at the same time, each with six pictures on their platform? How do you know their sense of humor? Or how they treat other people? Texting over dating apps can go on forever without any movement at all. It's always like:

> Hey, what are you up to tonight?

> Oh, not much, just like chilling with my roommate.

> Oh really? We should get together sometime.

> Yes!

And then maybe one of you tries to tell a joke and the other person is like, "Oh, that was weird," and then doesn't write back. Or the conversation just peters out because there's only so much to talk about with a person we know almost nothing about. We're wasting so much energy being indecisive and noncommittal and not wanting to take a chance and actually put time into someone we don't know. I talk to people all the time about online dating, and the frustrations are real. I get it, to a certain extent, because it feels like it take so much energy to go on another date with another guy and get dressed up and waste the time and get hopeful and then be disappointed.

But in a world forever changed by the pandemic, we have new options. We have new ways to get to know people. Everyone is on Zoom or can video chat with Facetime or WhatsApp. Overnight, Zoom became this platform everyone knew about, right? It went from this kind of techie platform that some businesses were using to everyone—even your grandma—Zooming.

On Zoom, you can literally match with someone on a dating app and you can meet them easily, and basically "live," without spending any money or even very much time. It's low stakes. But you can still find out if you click—are you attracted, is there chemistry there? You could also create an email just for that Zoom account, too, if you don't want to give out any of your personal information. You can say, "Hey, let's do a Zoom date tonight—I'd love to talk to you." Then you can hear their voice and see them and verify they're a real person. You can get someone's sense of humor in a video call. And you can keep it to five minutes or ten minutes or twenty minutes, whatever you want—or maybe it turns into a four-hour conversation. And at any point, if it's not going well, you can end it. You don't have to get the check or drive home—and they don't need to have any access to you whatsoever after that, either. It's all of the recon with none of the commitment.

And it's much easier to be charming when you have more rapport with someone. So you know, DM-ing a total stranger, you have zero rapport. After ten minutes on a Zoom call, you don't have a ton more rapport, but you have ten times more than you did before, and you know their body language, their voice—are they low energy or high energy?

What a great, fast, easy way to further check out someone that you're interested in. You liked their bio, you liked their picture, and you can find out a lot more about them in a twenty-minute Zoom call than you can with texting them over a dating app over the course of three to four weeks with no one really making any moves.

I told you how my current girlfriend, Natalie, and I met when she slid into my DMs. As I already mentioned, she was gorgeous, and that piqued my curiosity enough to reply. I wasn't like, "Oh, I'm in love with this woman." I was like, "Wow." And then I immediately started thinking to myself, *Should I write back, should I not? I don't know.* And I joke that we're living in a world where people get catfished, but we are. So I messaged her, and she messaged me back, "Oh, what's your Snapchat?" Snapchat had a video call feature you could use, but the beauty of doing it this way was that the other person wouldn't have access to your number. So I called her, because I wanted to see if she was real. I was like, if she picks up, she's legit. And then she picked up. I said, "Show me your ID"—romantic, I know—but as I said, catfishing is a real thing.

Luckily Natalie has an amazing personality, but there are a lot of pretty people I've met who suck, you know? And I might have decided that she sucked. I could have talked to her, and two hours or two days in realized I was ready to move on. It's really easy for us to decide whether or not we're physically attracted to a person, but you definitely shouldn't be thinking of that as an indicator of whether or not there's something deeper there. At the beginning, you shouldn't even get that excited. You can be like, it's nice that I'm interested in this person physically, but then you have to go from there.

SHOOTING YOUR SHOT WITH A FRIEND

So, you think you have feelings for your close friend. Maybe you think you're in love with them. You're just not sure if you should "risk" the friendship by making the first move and finding out if they feel the same way.

Well, you should know that this friendship has an expiration date. The current friendship you find yourself in is going to end. Either you'll be in a romantic relationship with this person, which is different, or one of you finally meets someone else and you no longer have the time to give to the friendship you once did.

Chances are, this friendship has all the things a romantic relationship has without the romance. You talk every day, you hang out, go to dinner, and they're the first person you talk to when you need to solve a problem. You just don't have sex. The biggest reason why this friendship even blossomed is that you were single and had the space in your life to invest your time in someone who was just a friend. Or maybe you never really wanted to be their friend, but deep down you were just too scared to take the risk of getting rejected. So a friendship was a safer option that still allowed you to have them in your life.

Knowing that it's going to end, or at least not stay the same way indefinitely, you might as well take a chance. Be honest, communicate with them, and let them know how you feel: You never know, it might just end with a happily ever after.

STOP WARNING YOUR CRUSH

Let's say your friend crush is now chasing someone you think is one of the "bad ones"—a player, or maybe just a fuckboy—and you know you're one of the good ones. It's not your place to let them know. This is not a way to shoot your shot, and this will only decrease the chances of them ever considering you as an option. Your friend crush probably is already aware of the risks they are taking. Your comment will annoy them by making them feel they aren't smart enough to notice, or worse, make them feel judged for making bad choices. Neither of which makes you look more attractive to them. It will often backfire, and make them feel even closer to the person you are warning them about. Why? Because you're giving your friend crush an opportunity to feel special. Your comments give their ego a chance to stand out, maybe even to make them feel like they're better than the other people who weren't good enough for the fuckboy they are chasing. And then, even if your crush goes to the person they're chasing with questions about any of the valid concerns you might have brought up, you are just providing that not-good person an opportunity to say some fuckboy or player shit to your crush, who is already primed to believe whatever that person says. Instead, eventually try honesty about your own feelings for them, as I've already explained above.

A FINAL NOTE: YOUR RELATIONSHIP
WON'T CARE HOW YOU MET

"Oh my god, how did you two meet?" This is a common question someone is asked when revealing to their friends that they are dating someone new. This detail has been engrained in our minds as something that matters by rom-coms. It is commonly known as the "meet-cute." While the meet-cute makes for a compelling moment in any love story, it's not an indicator of the likelihood of success in the relationship. It's nothing more than an anecdote to talk about at lunch with your friend or a conversation starter at a party. Your relationship doesn't care. It won't impact how well you communicate with each other, how empathetic you are with one another, or how deeply you feel. The only really significant impact of a compelling meetup story is that you might ignore real issues about your compatibility early on, because you put too much value on fate and that great story about how you met. When you're out there dating and trying to meet your person, don't worry about how you two met.

How Natalie and I met isn't a romantic story on its own. She sent me a message, I responded. We video-chatted, we ended up meeting up in NYC. We both laugh now because when we first met in person, we knew very little about one another and both thought the other was kind of crazy for even agreeing to meet. When we get asked how we met, we just tell the truth. There is no judgment. No one really has an opinion. And if they did, we wouldn't care. For us, it just makes sense.

Yet so many people fantasize about meeting someone in a more romantic way, hoping to be able to tell a story that sounds something like, "We were the only two in a coffee shop and this song came on and he asked me to dance, but when he walked over he slipped and fell and I had to rush him to the hospital to get stitches and now we are in love." Sure I guess that would make for a fun story, but it doesn't speak to long-term compatibility at all. So many people will embellish how they met or even make up a story because they don't want to admit they met on a dating app. If you're looking to date and meet new people, don't judge the different ways you could meet someone. There is nothing wrong with trying. There is nothing worth having in your life if you don't have to try to get it. Be open to all the possibilities that could bring you something positive. A romantic meet-cute isn't what makes a relationship work. Judging how you might meet someone can only limit your chances of something positive happening.

We all want that fairy-tale story. But you have to remember that the thing that truly makes the fairy tale is the happy ending, not the "Once upon a time."

QUESTIONS WITH NICK

Q:

Met a guy on Bumble but having a hard time with the fact that we met on Bumble. Advice?

A:

That's like having a hard time with the fact that you were served food to eat at a restaurant.

Q:

Dating profile tips! Help! Less is more or clever and short bio?

A:

It should read: "If you like my face, then buy me a drink so I can figure out whether or not I like your personality and give you a chance to like mine."

Q:

I messed up time and time again with my best friend. I've owned up to it and apologized. But he's leaving my life and I will do anything to save this friendship. What do I do?

A:

We are lucky to get second chances. There has never been a third chance that was deserved. If your track record is that bad, it might be too late with this friend. Which for you might be the best thing. So you can really learn and be a better friend to someone else in the future.

QUESTIONS WITH NICK

Q:

Best friend hooks up with gross girls, but friendzones me. Say something or forget him?

A:

I think you should stop calling your crush your best friend. And then move on.

Q:

Can you get out of the friend zone?

A:

To get something you want you must be willing to lose something. If you don't want to be "just friends," then stop being friends without also getting the relationship and sex. Then start dating someone else. Let them see you in a different light.

Q:

How do you shoot your shot successfully?

A:

By not being afraid to miss.

Q:

Tips for someone just starting college, trying to meet people and fit in?

A:

Don't try to fit in, find things you enjoy doing, and make friends with those people who are enjoying the same thing.

CHAPTER 4

THE
FIRST
DATE

THE BIGGEST MISTAKE PEOPLE
MAKE ON FIRST DATES

The biggest mistake people make on first dates is that they focus all their energy on making sure their date likes them, instead of focusing on whether or not they are even interested in a second date. While it's important to get that kind of validation from the people we love, what about the people we aren't interested in loving? Sure, in a perfect world, everyone would like us, but the world isn't perfect. So why are we wasting our energy worrying if a date is going to like us, when we don't even know if we like them?

We all have insecurities and baggage about things—maybe limited sexual experience, maybe vast sexual experience, maybe mental health struggles, body image issues, problematic family, or our attachment to our pets. Add social media into the mix, and our insecurities become even more magnified because everyone presents their perfect self. When we are single and we are dating, we have a tendency to worry about those insecurities and that baggage, and the things we do that annoy other people, and we try to hide them, which then prevents us from being accepted—or loved—for who we actually are. After all, what is love if not feeling accepted and safe while being our truest selves? It's those annoying habits that many of us will put in maximum effort to keep contained and out of sight while we are getting to know someone. But that worry—and desire for acceptance—causes us to focus on the wrong things when it comes to first dates.

Now, I'm not bringing this up to say that you're wasting your time being on your best behavior. Especially when we are in social settings, it's good to be polite, well-behaved, and attentive to the people around you. First dates can be stressful, and they're often with people who are strangers, so, whether you end up liking them or not, you should be respectful of each other's time. You should want them to enjoy themself even if there isn't a shared romantic interest when the date is over.

But consider that you might end up being in a relationship with this person. While it is important to be on your best behavior, it's just as important to be yourself. Being yourself on first dates has a lot to do with honestly answering the questions you're being asked. You should be authentic, which also means putting zero thought into whether or not your date will agree with you.

I always tell people to put no thought into what you're going to say about yourself. You know yourself better than anyone, so all you have to do is answer the questions they ask about you. It's not your job to come in on a first or second date prepared to tell an amazing story about yourself. A first date is not meant to be a prepared presentation that conveys everything about you. A first date is you trying to get to know someone else. Instead of worrying about what you'll say, keep things as simple as possible and just focus your energy on deciding whether or not you're interested in having a second date. I feel we can all agree that that sounds a heck of a lot less stressful than fixating on being liked or accepted by someone we barely know.

I'm sure you're hoping your date is as honest with you as you are with them. Best-case scenario, both parties are being their truest selves, giving their date a chance to fairly consider whether or not there is genuine interest.

Even if you think I'm nuts for saying you shouldn't worry about whether or not your date likes you, the good news is that we live in a world where honest people—honest but considerate people—are nearly always considered attractive. Being honest takes a lot of confidence. What's the sign of a really confident person on a first date? To me, it's not having all this bravado or peacocking or hitting on the other person, it's being honest about who you are and putting that energy out there. This is true at every point in a relationship too, because honestly acknowledging your insecurities, and honestly acknowledging that you have things to work on, is part of a healthy relationship. It's scary to put yourself out there to people and let them judge you, and doing so is a real sign of confidence. Much of the time, when people are honest and confident with their answers, the person listening is charmed by the authenticity they're seeing. And if they don't like what they're hearing, they weren't your person anyway. So really owning who you are is always a win-win.

But we should also remember that honesty is an art form, right? The words "I'm just being honest" are not an excuse to say anything and everything you want. Sometimes you can be too honest and hurt people's feelings needlessly.

Maybe it goes without saying, but while you should be yourself and you should be honest about who you are, there is also an appropriate time to share deeper insecurities and your darkest secrets with the person you're dating, and the first date is not that time. The first date is about being honest about who you are, but it's not the time or place to share all your truth. Your job is not to unload. You don't go on a first date and meet someone and just say, "You know, these are my bad habits"—plus, you also don't know what they're going to like or dislike about you, or what they consider bad habits. The first date is more about making sure you don't waste your time sharing that personal information with someone that you won't be seeing again in the future.

And this is getting to the primary reason we should be honest about who we are: A first date is about the possibility of finding love. Or at least finding like that can turn into love. It isn't about running a campaign where you are trying to get as many people to like you as possible. This is about finding one person. One person to last you a lifetime. In order for that to be possible, we need to let the people we meet know who we are.

Listen, I get asked this question all the time: "I've had so many really nice first dates, but I never can get a second date or a third date. Is something wrong with me?" I say if every second date ends with you wanting a third date, then you're breaking the first rule of dating—be yourself. Most likely you're coming across as someone who just wants to be liked, instead of whoever you really are. If you are thinking about your boundaries and what you want and looking for people who are worthy of your time and being honest about who you are—there's just not that many compatible people in this world for you to always want the second or third date.

But I promise you, there are plenty of people looking for someone just like you. That doesn't mean they won't ever find you annoying. It just means that what they love about you will far outweigh the things that drive them crazy. If you're too busy always pretending to be someone you think other people will like more, then the people who want to love you might miss you. There will be a lot of people interested in you that you won't find all that appealing and vice versa. It's hard to find that match, so don't make it any harder than it needs to be. Embrace your insecurities. Acknowledge your bad habits with the promise to always try to work on them. Don't pretend to be someone you're not. Even the best actors can't do method for a lifetime.

GETTING THE MOST OUT OF A FIRST DATE

Here are my ideas on how to get the most out of a first date. Think about all of the below on your next first date. Now you can go into those first dates stress free. Go in more confident, and more adventurous. Be curious and be observant, knowing you have nothing to lose but a few hours spent getting to know someone else.

 Ask questions.

If your only goal on a first date is to get to know the other person well enough to be able to determine whether or not you're interested in a second date, then all you really need to focus on during the date are the questions you want to ask them.

Your only job on a first date is to ask questions and follow-up questions, listen to the answers you're getting, and answer the questions you're asked honestly.

Doesn't that just make the date an interview? Well, yes, the first date is an interview. I know people don't like to think of it that way, they really hate that metaphor, but that doesn't invalidate the idea, or the process. Think about a successful job interview—it is when both parties prioritize making sure that the potential relationship would be mutually beneficial. With a job interview, the employee wants an opportunity to make money and gain experience. The employer wants to hire someone who will bring value through the work they accomplish. Many—maybe most—job interviews are unsuccessful because there is too often an uneven power dynamic. Either the position is highly competitive, or the candidate is extremely sought after by multiple employers. When the power dynamic is unequal, the party that has less power has a tendency to overperform and be inauthentic in order to win the approval of the person in power. This almost always leads to future disappointment by either one or both parties involved. When the power dynamic is even, the interest in learning about one another can be reciprocal. The questions flow both ways, and the answers are more likely to be authentic.

Unlike with jobs, dating prospects are virtually unlimited, so what I mainly want you to do is relieve the pressure of preparing for the interview, and evening out the power dynamic. The pressure should essentially be zero.

Some people will say, "Well then, I end up talking the whole time because they didn't ask me questions." If the person isn't asking you questions that prompt an opportunity to talk about yourself, then they could be shy or nervous, true, but it could also be a sign that maybe they're self-centered, or maybe they're not all that interested in you now and maybe they never will be, because they're just kind of interested in themselves. Or maybe they're not interesting in the way you would need a partner to be. If you're on a date and you're the only one asking questions, that means one of two things: Either they are uninterested in learning more about you or they are too concerned with seeking your validation. Either way, that's a pretty good indicator that there isn't a future.

2 Pay attention to what your date asks you.

We can learn a lot about someone by the questions they ask, so pay attention to the things they are interested in learning. When we know very little about someone, the questions should be broad in order to give space to the person answering, allowing them to answer in a way that makes them feel most comfortable. If one person's questions are more specific off the bat, then that's a clear sign that a topic is a high priority to them. If their question is "When was the last time you had sex?," then what they are most interested in is how likely you are to have sex with them, or in gauging how "promiscuous" they think you are and making a judgment based on that. The only reason questions should get specific on a first date is that the conversation goes there naturally. Both people are equally participating in both asking and answering questions. The specificity should make sense. If the person you're on a date with asks a question that comes out of nowhere, pay very close attention to what the question is because it gives a big clue about their motives.

Don't freak out if they don't seem excited. In some cases, not being excited isn't a bad thing. For example, most first dates are just in-person meet-ups for two people who met on dating apps, each of whom could have eight other text conversations going on with eight other people they have matched with. While it's always nice to have someone be excited about you, it's often the case that on first dates both people are debating whether or not they should stay for a second drink, let alone consider planning a second date. In many cases, you've never even talked to this person: How excited can you be about someone you have only seen a few pictures of and had a few text conversations with?

Most dates are going to be with people you're not going to want to end up with, but I also think people need to stop avoiding second dates just because they didn't fall in love on the first date. You know, *Oh, there wasn't a spark*. But sometimes the spark is just they were tall and hot. Well, that's not necessarily a good thing, right? That just means you want to like them, but you don't know anything about them.

3 Don't feel obligated to answer any super personal questions.

After all, you're talking to a stranger. Why the fuck would you tell a stranger your deepest darkest secrets or most sensitive personal details? Another reason to make sure your focus is on getting to know that person, instead of seeking their validation. Someone with a sincere interest in getting to know you will want to start at the beginning. They know nothing about you, so even your answers to the most basic questions will be interesting. Plus, we should only share our biggest insecurities with the people we trust, and we can't possibly trust someone we know very little about.

4 Don't lie.

Hopefully this is already very clear, but don't tell big lies like "I am fine with just hooking up" if you're not—and definitely don't tell little white lies to make the person like you more, which happens a lot on first dates. They like golf/video games/surfing/shopping/cooking and you don't? Don't just say you like it too. What can you say instead? "Hey, listen, I'm like not a big fan of that, but I really love doing xyz." Or "I don't know much about that, but I'd be up for checking it out." Or "That's not really my thing, but I think it's great that you get into it with your friends." This is also an opportunity for you to learn more about the other person. You can ask what drew them to that particular interest. If it's something you're not interested in, rather than pretend you are, you would be much better served to admit it's not your thing, but that you appreciate it when people in a relationship have separate interests.

The desire to lie in this situation might be born of a fear of showing the other person something about yourself that they don't like, or an insecurity about your potential differences. But that's all the more reason why being honest is so important. Those differences will always reveal themselves one way or the other. I think what's more important than finding out that you have the exact same general interests as this person is finding out what kind of partner they would be—not just how they spend their free time, but how they react to things, how you spend your free time, or the idea you do or don't like things, or do or don't want to spend all of your free time with your partner. The main point is, if you're being honest—but polite—about what you don't have a genuine interest in and what you're willing to do and how much you'd like to share and intertwine your life, that's a much more authentic way of getting to know someone. Maybe your answers might be something they don't want to hear and again, that is okay, because again, your goal isn't to get them to like you, but to decide if you like them.

5 **Simplify your moments.**

When I say simplify your moments, I mean stop making things more important than they need to be. Remember that they are not supposed to fall in love with you on the first date. They are not supposed to sweep you off your feet on the first date. They are just trying to get to know you, and hopefully be themselves. After all, you may or may not like them, either, right? So go on the dates, focus on having fun, stop worrying about if they like you, stop trying to analyze every exchange, stop trying to figure out what something means. You're putting too much pressure on yourself, and subsequently your first dates. This probably sounds repetitive, but it's worth repeating because so many of us make this mistake.

QUESTIONS WITH NICK

Q:

Girl I like has a boyfriend but I think I'm better for her . . . what do I do?

A:

It's her call what's best for her. Be your best self and your best match will eventually find you.

Q:

My boyfriend died last year. I'm starting to date again. Do you think that's a turnoff?

A:

I'm sorry for your loss. Not unless you killed him.

Q:

Hard time opening up to new guys due to trust issues (my ex cheated). Any advice?

A:

Trust is a choice. The new guys are not your ex. So, choose to be trusting, rather than resentful. You only give your ex more power by letting him impact your feelings in new relationships.

QUESTIONS WITH NICK

Q:

Why has feeling not cute enough or good enough become something so common?

A:

Because we have too much access and ability to constantly compare ourselves to others.

Q:

Do you believe that time heals all wounds?

A:

Sure, but it doesn't mean it still won't leave scars.

Q:

Advice on being patient for finding Mr. Right?

A:

Even Mr. Right will get on your nerves at some point during forever. So why rush it?

QUESTIONS WITH NICK

Q:

No boy at college is going to want to date me because I'm still a virgin. How will I ever find someone?

A:

People love people who believe in their choices. Believe in yours. Plenty of people will want to date you for your conviction. Not everyone will want to, but you don't want everyone or just anyone.

Q:

Any advice on gaining confidence?

A:

Pick something about yourself that you're insecure about. Something that you would prefer people not know. Then admit it to someone. You will find their reaction won't be nearly as bad as you had imagined. You will do something brave, and you will survive it. Making you realize there are many more things you're capable of.

Q:

Incredible first date. More nervous now for date 2. How to chill/be present?

A:

You know maybe 1% about them with 99% left to learn, but you're acting like you have nothing else to focus on other than hoping they like you. Focus on learning more about the 99% of them you don't know about, that should keep you present for a while.

CHAPTER 5

HOW TO GET BETTER AT DATING

NEVER STOP LEARNING

Something I've talked about a lot on my podcasts recently is that I think we often make the mistake of going out with someone on a first or second date, and then essentially checking off all the boxes on some lists we have in our heads. They're attractive. They have a job that's cool. And then we'll think to ourselves, *We had a pretty good date, I had a really nice time, I had a lot of fun.* And that fun might just be a result of the restaurant or the sunset, or maybe it was different from the past relationship you just got out of, or this was the best date you've been on after a series of comically bad dates. And so for all intents and purposes, you did have a really nice time with that person.

Then you'll tell yourself, *Hey, I like this person.* And it is amazing how many people, from that moment forward, stop getting to know that new someone. Now they want to like that person, and they will literally stop learning about that person. Once they think they like someone, now all they're trying to do is just like them more.

Yet the reaction after a good date or few dates should be, *I think I like this person, but, if I'm being honest, I have so much more to learn about them, so I'm going to be optimistic, but we still have to see.* But instead, many people decide that they're not going to ask any questions that might peel back a layer they won't like—that it's better to just lean into all the things they like so far, and ignore all the rest. When you spell it out that way, it seems like insane behavior. Yet, I think that's by far the norm. Often once we decide that we like someone, we'll just stop learning. But you can be both excited about the potential and aware that you still have so much to learn. The key is knowing that if you learn something you don't like, it might be the end of the possibility of that relationship, but it's not the end of the world.

I made this exact mistake with my second serious relationship. My first serious girlfriend and I fought about religion a lot. I'm not the same anymore—my views on religion and its importance in my relationships have changed—but I was raised in a very Catholic family, and church was still very important to me when I was just out of high school, and she had a lot of issues with religion in general. When we finally broke up, in large part due to that friction, I met a girl who was just as beautiful and confident as my ex, except she also went to church every Sunday. And I was immediately, "Oh my God, I love you." She had a bunch of qualities that were similar to those of my first girlfriend. *And* she was okay with going to church.

That is a very common story: You have a relationship that didn't work out, and then you go on a first date with someone you're attracted to, and they don't do this one thing your ex always did. And that's it—it's boom, you're in love.

In reality, my second serious girlfriend and I had almost nothing in common. It took a while for me to see it, but we didn't really enjoy spending time with each other, and we didn't have a ton of fun together. But I didn't care at the time, because I had put so much weight on her being religious. Once I saw that she had some superficial qualities I liked—I was attracted to her, she went to church—I stopped asking more questions. I didn't pay any attention to our compatibility, and whether we enjoyed being around each other.

And you could replace "religion" with almost any trait or activity that you personally love at any point in time. Say I was a huge Green Bay Packers fan and my first girlfriend hated sports. And we fought over sports all the time— I wanted her to like them, she hated them. She told me sports were stupid. And then my next girlfriend was like, "I love sports. Can I be on your fantasy football team?" I'd be so happy about that that I don't even realize we don't really connect in all kinds of other ways, or that I don't like all kinds of other things about them.

In dating situations like these, people are not asking enough questions. They think, *I don't want to be interviewing.* Or they do ask questions, and don't listen to the answers—we all make that mistake sometimes. We'll ask questions and we're not even listening to the answers because truth is, we just want to like the other person. You meet a beautiful woman, and you think, *Oh, she's so beautiful.* She tells one joke and you're like, *Hot and fun?* Or you go on a date with a much younger person than you'd normally go out with, and she says one wise thing and you think, *Oh, she's super mature for her age.*

But in real life, you have to be willing to find out that they're not fun or mature—you have to ask questions and you have to be willing to hear the answers and figure out they're not your person. The real problem isn't whether you like them right now, but whether you're going to like them in a year. But we often don't do that—we decide we like them now, and we don't want them to say too much to ruin it.

Sometimes it's the reverse that's true. Instead of deciding we like someone because they're attractive and have a nice job and forgetting to pay attention to any other details, we don't learn enough to realize that there's real potential there. Say we feel a little discouraged after a first date—you know, it was nice, but they were kind of awkward and you didn't leave super excited, but it wasn't bad or totally boring, maybe there was no quote-unquote spark. Well then, why not go on a second or third date? I know it doesn't feel like it felt when you hooked up with your first boyfriend or girlfriend, and you had never felt sparks before. It felt so new and foreign and magical, and, yeah, I get that. But if you've learned anything from the chapter on training our pickers (page 34), it's that maybe you hadn't been so great at choosing second dates in the past. Why not be patient and get to know someone who wasn't so bad a little more before you dismiss them totally? After all, what's one more date in the search for your person?

REMEMBER THAT EVERYONE IS ANNOYING

I hate it when I go on social media and I see an oversimplified list of things to avoid in a dating profile or once you've been on a first date. I'm exaggerating a little, maybe, but usually that list includes things like "too many tattoos" or "hates cats." Maybe those lists are meant to be satirical and funny, but since I am hoping to give people good advice that gets them more of what they want, I avoid those types of lists because the things on them are usually pet peeves, not non-negotiables.

To refresh your memory, pet peeves are things you should be able to live with in an otherwise good relationship, while non-negotiables are the things you wouldn't want to live with in any relationship at all. Here's a story to illustrate what I mean. I have a girlfriend—as in a friend who is a woman—who has no problem at all getting dates because she's confident and fun and interesting and beautiful. But she's also constantly cycling through those guys—and she is always the one who breaks up with them. Recently she said something to me like, "I just don't know what my problem is with dating."

I said to her, "You treat your pet peeves like non-negotiables. Everything's a big deal with you. If you find something annoying about a guy—they're late, or disagree with you, or don't want to go to the same movie, or don't like that kind of restaurant—you just freak out and break up with them."

In my friend's mind, almost anything that isn't exactly as she hoped or planned is a non-negotiable.

(If you're tempted to tell a friend in a similar situation the same thing, consider this: Something that I've learned as someone who gives advice to people for a living is that if someone isn't interested in getting advice, if they're not actually interested in hearing it, then they're not going to receive it well. Sometimes, I'll just tell people, "I don't know if you really want my advice, because if you want my advice, I'm gonna tell you what I really think." When people call in on my show, it often works, because they're literally taking the time to call in. They've reached a point where they're done hearing what they want to hear or being placated by family and friends. But they have to be ready for that—and if they're not ready for that, they don't want to hear it.)

How often do you get sick of a friend and think to yourself, *I just need a few days, then it'll be fine—they do that annoying thing, but I still love them.* You don't have to tell them that, you know what I'm saying? We easily get space and a break from our friends, and we often easily put up with their annoying habits. Some people, when they deal with the same type of thing from someone they're dating, tend to panic. The person you're in love with is not supposed to annoy you at all, right?

I told my friend what I always say, which is to remember that everyone is annoying. We all get on someone else's nerves from time to time. As I said before, even greatness can be annoying. Instead of panicking when you come across something annoying, you have to decide what's really important. Is that really a non-negotiable, or is it a pet peeve? There are many cases where maybe it's best to wait and see, or to pay more attention to the behavior that's bothering you before you make a decision. Let's say you're on a third or fourth date, and you've realized that on your first date they were fifteen minutes late, and on your second date they were five minutes late, and on your fourth date they were ten minutes late. And now you realize that this person is maybe just one of those people who's always just a little late.

You have to consider whether ten, fifteen, twenty minutes is really the end of the world. What if you're having an amazing time and really enjoy their company, but they're just not good at managing their time. Maybe you could definitely learn to live with that right now. But you might also think to yourself, *Okay, well, is this person being their best self? When they get really comfortable with me, are they going to start being an hour late? Will they literally be on their couch when I am at the restaurant? I don't need to break up. I don't need to end this thing because they are slightly inconsiderate with their time. I don't love that, but maybe I don't need to freak out.* Maybe you just pay more attention. It's a yellow flag—a warning. You're like, *All right, I need to pay attention to this. I maybe need to ask some questions around this topic to see how big of an issue this is. Are they willing to work on this with me? Can I adjust?* Maybe it's just a matter of telling them to get to the restaurant at 7 P.M. when you're actually planning to get there at 7:15.

Now sometimes things are both annoying and an obvious non-negotiable. If you're on a first, or second, or third date with someone and they're being a dick to your server at a restaurant, that's a real red flag. This person couldn't even pretend to be nice in front of someone they're still trying to impress—that's a potential indicator of a real character flaw and thus a non-negotiable.

Behavior that's equally self-destructive as my friend thinking everything is a non-negotiable is putting up with some non-negotiables as if they're pet peeves. Like sticking around when someone doesn't speak to you with respect, or putting up with recurring infidelity or anger. Some people talk themselves into believing those are annoying habits, instead of what they are: real reasons to leave a relationship.

BE HONEST ABOUT NON-NEGOTIABLES

We all love to romanticize the idea that someone will love us so much that they will be willing to move for us, to give up a job they worked decades to get, or overlook differences in religion or age. But that really depends on the person. For some people, they might be so close with their family and friends that their local community is a huge part of who they are. To move would be taking all of that away from this person. That's really hard to justify, and that might be a legitimate non-negotiable—but people convince themselves that they might one day be able to do it, that they can live with it, and after many years of long-distance dating, they finally realize moving away from their daily support system was actually a non-negotiable.

Not understanding my own non-negotiables (see page 23) was the problem with my first serious relationship. I grew up in a very traditional Catholic household, and religion was a big part of my life when I was younger. I went to church every Sunday, and a bulk of my parents' marriage and relationship was centered around religion. They were literally introduced by a Catholic priest. The church was great for them and I really respected their relationship, so I wanted to emulate it. When I was a young man—a nineteen-, twenty-year-old man—I thought I wanted that in a relationship too. My very first girlfriend, she was raised as a Catholic too, but her family just wasn't very religious at all. And quite frankly, she wasn't comfortable with religion, and she was clear about her feelings.

Still, we would fight about religion a lot. Back then, I really thought I was doing the right thing by saying, "This is important to me, and if you want to be with me, if you want to share your life with me, I need you to share this with me too." And she felt just the opposite, which left us as two people trying to navigate a big difference in the way we saw our lives.

Looking back, I can clearly see that at that point in my life, maybe I should have been thinking of religion as a non-negotiable, as it is for many people. If you are in fact super religious, that is a very big deal, and it's going to be a big part of your life. And even though my girlfriend and I ultimately split up, by treating this huge issue as something that could be resolved, even though our stances on it were in direct opposition to one another, we both endured a lot of fighting and heartache that we could have avoided.

As I mentioned in the section on situationships (page 49), there is nothing wrong with taking risks and being vulnerable in a situation that may not work out the way you hope. Just don't lie to yourself about the situation—be honest with yourself about what you're trying to do and what you want, and be honest about the effort that it will require and the risks.

Whether you're trying to make a long-distance relationship work, or date someone much older or younger than you are or with different views, just be realistic about these situations. Don't approach them with the mindset that it's just meant to be. Each of those situations I described will have more challenges and hurdles than dating someone who lives in the same city, or is closer to your age, and you should be honest with yourself about that.

DON'T JUDGE PEOPLE FOR HAVING
A LONG LIST OF EXES

I am sure many of you are saying to yourselves, *What? Me? Judge? I would never.* Many of you might even be telling the truth. Still, think about it for a second. We romanticize love all the time. We idealize being someone's first love. With that romanticization comes judgment for people who might have had a few, or even many, past partners.

I like to use the dream house analogy: Your idea of a dream house might change over time, right? What you thought you wanted just out of college is probably different than your dream house when you're thirty-two. Maybe you wanted a house just like the one you grew up in, or the one next door. But over the years you've traveled, and been invited over to all kinds of houses you've never been in before. All of a sudden your original dream house doesn't seem to be such a dream anymore. It's the same with the person who's had just one or two partners as opposed to someone who has dated a dozen people: The person with more experience probably has learned a lot more about what they really want in a relationship.

When that person says "I love you," you're going to feel confident about those words and what they mean to that person, because they'll be clearer from experience what those words really mean. So instead of seeing multiple past partners as a negative, instead of wanting to be someone's first and only, be thankful that they've had that experience with other people already.

If you're still feeling nervous, ask questions and talk to them about those relationships before you commit to one with them yourself. You could ask them, "What's something about past relationships you've had that you never want to replicate?" Or "What's something about a past relationship that you hope to have again?" They should be able to offer both kinds of examples.

With that in mind, I asked my audience if they judge people if they've had a lot of exes—whatever "a lot" meant to them. Here are the results: 36 percent admitted to passing judgment on someone if they thought they had a lot of exes. Given that we live in a world full of judgment and we often judge more than we like to admit, I'm going to assume the real number is actually a little higher. Still, even 36 percent feels high, especially when you consider the fact that the people being judged are likely just putting themselves out there and trying to find their person. If you want to start making dating less confusing for yourself, start by not judging others for taking risks on the path to finding their person.

MAKING SEX TIMELINES ONLY WASTES YOUR TIME

I get these questions all the time: Should I sleep with someone on a first date? How long should you wait to have sex with someone? I hate those questions because I don't care whether you have sex on the first date or third date or five months later, I just want you to set expectations and boundaries first, like I discussed at the beginning of the book and as we'll touch on in the chapter on hookup culture (see page 128). Instead, some people set timelines for people they are dating. Often these timelines are based solely on the premise that if you make someone wait, they will respect you more, see you as more of a challenge, and will therefore be more interested in having a serious relationship with you. But making someone wait for the sake of waiting will have no impact on the level of emotional connection they have with you.

There is a common misconception about dating—that someone might lose respect for you if you have sex "too soon." When people have sex within the first few dates and one seems to lose interest shortly after, many people will claim that the other person lost interest because they started judging the person for having sex with them too soon. Some people will make the mistake of judging themselves, beating themselves up emotionally, wondering if that person would still be in the picture had they waited longer. For anyone out there who has ever once judged themselves for having sex too soon, I want you to know that making them wait wouldn't have made a bit of difference. Stop judging yourself, because I can promise you, they aren't doing so themselves.

I hope that makes you feel better, because the next part might sting a tad. They lost interest not because they think differently of you, but because they just aren't interested in having sex with you again. To help explain this reality, I'm going to use the Movie Theory to articulate how some people process sex.

When people watch a movie, they tend to have one of three experiences. They either hate the movie and have a hard time getting through it, enjoy the movie but are satisfied with only seeing the movie one time, or love the movie and look forward to watching it over and over. Movies that we love are few and far between, but when we love them, we will always enjoy seeing them again. This is how a lot of people process sex.

Most of the time, they have a nice time because sex is generally an enjoyable thing, like how a movie is generally an enjoyable thing; they just have no real desire to see it again. However, if someone really enjoys having sex with you, I promise you will hear from them again. Like a great movie, great sex isn't easy to find. If you hooked up with somebody and didn't hear from them, or they ended things shortly after, it's because they decided that sex with you is totally okay, but not interesting enough to want to do it again. I know it's tough hearing that, but it's a hell of a lot better than thinking they're judging you for doing something wrong. Or, possibly, they did enjoy having sex with you, but they know they don't want anything more and *hopefully* you've set clear boundaries that you do.

And it also doesn't imply that you're bad in bed, just simply that you two don't mesh well together, for any number of reasons.

It's extremely important to note that just because someone likes having sex with you doesn't necessarily mean they like you. I would go so far as to say that people are fully capable of loving sex with someone they don't even enjoy being around. This can only last so long, as eventually the amount of time you have to spend with them won't be worth it, but early on, it's easy to ignore that.

So how can you tell if that's what's happening? It's not that hard, actually. First, knowing that it's possible is half the battle, because now you can pay attention to how this person treats you in between having sex. You can review the list of traits for fuckboys (page 40) and players (page 45), but some common signs of someone loving having sex with you but not enjoying your company are all those "you up?" texts late at night, last-minute plans, leaving immediately after sex, or saying they have an early morning so they can't stay over.

Again, when you set up timelines thinking the longer a person is willing to stick around the more sincere they are, you are setting yourself up for major disappointment. You should be setting expectations and boundaries—that's how you avoid disappointment. You're not building an emotional connection just by challenging anyone to see how long they are willing to wait to have sex with you. Without an emotional connection, you're probably going to get the same result you would get if you had sex with them on night one as you would get on month four.

PRIORITIZE THE BOUNDARIES YOU SET
OVER CHEMISTRY YOU FEEL

When it comes to dating and looking for "the one," many of us rely on feeling chemistry or a natural connection to let us know when we've found someone worth exploring. Chemistry is a real thing. It's that intangible feeling of magnetic attraction that really begins the initial fascination you may have with a person. However, the thing about chemistry is that it's very hard to trust its potential. It may immediately fizzle out after that first intoxicating flare of lust. Some people are just more naturally charismatic, and we all tend to feel a sort of instant connection with them. Perhaps they are thrillingly present or possess that larger-than-life aura, or maybe they are just naturally gifted at relating to people. Chemistry can also be manufactured when certain aspects of our environments are controlled. As someone who spent a lot of time focusing on love in a reality TV environment, I can assure you that when you have a singular focus and a limited supply of anything, it's not that hard to start feeling all sorts of chemistry with people. Sure, most of you won't experience a controlled environment as radical as you find on *The Bachelor*, but other common things can bring an element of control to our environments—one that narrows your focus and limits your options. Such things as having similar friends, being members at the same church, or shared experiences can all make it a little easier to feel chemistry with certain people. Our egos also can play a role in our confusing chemistry with an opportunity to feel validation. Is it chemistry we are feeling, or is this person we find incredibly attractive just giving us a little attention? Despite its being unreliable and potentially manufactured, sadly, it's still very hard to find. As a result, when we experience it with someone, we tend to overvalue its importance when it comes to determining whether that person is worthy of our time and attention.

When people call in to my podcast to tell me about a dating situation they are struggling with, they will often list off many challenges they are having, but then attempt to justify the relationship through how much chemistry they have with this person. They give me a list of all the things they don't like: "They are inconsistent"; "They say they don't want a relationship"; "When they get mad, they can be mean"—but always follow up with a very loud and confident "BUT WE HAVE SO MUCH CHEMISTRY." Chemistry with someone is a great feeling, and it can certainly make dating easier and a lot more fun early on, but too many of us will use that feeling of chemistry to ignore the boundaries we try to set for ourselves. Chemistry is a part of falling in love, but it's just one of many factors. It is also something that can grow over time as you start building an emotional connection. We must be careful not to use it as an excuse to start negotiating with ourselves about the standards and boundaries we work so hard to establish. Standards and boundaries that we know we will need for us to feel happy and loved in the long run—don't disregard a solid emotional base in favor of a fleeting infatuation. So, the next time you feel that chemistry, enjoy it; just be mindful not to use it as an excuse to look the other way when things start feeling a little off.

UNLEASH THE POWER OF DEFINING THE RELATIONSHIP

You can think of defining a relationship as maybe a step beyond setting expectations and boundaries, though those things are involved. Defining the relationship is just talking through those two things with the person you are dating. When do I think people should define the relationship? Whenever you feel like you want or need more from your relationship, whenever you're confused about the expectations of your relationship, or whenever you're in a situation where you want to get some clarity. You can define your relationship after a few weeks, after a few months, or after a few years—whenever you need to, or whenever things change.

Defining the relationship could be "I don't want to see other people and I was hoping you feel the same." Maybe it's "I think I'd like to move in with you, and I am hoping you feel the same." Maybe it's caused by the fact that you've just had sex with the person you're dating, and now you want to keep doing that, but you'd prefer that they're not sleeping with other people. Defining the relationship can be as simple as agreeing to put a pause on dating other people while you focus on each other, all while agreeing to check in in a couple weeks to see how it's going.

I actually gave my podcast audience a poll about when it made sense to first define a relationship, and I gave them two options. Do you first define your relationship when you reach:

Option A: The point when you are confident in your feelings for the other person?

or

Option B: The point when you like the person enough that you want to get to know them better, and set boundaries and definitions around not sleeping with other people, in the hopes that things will progress?

The results were essentially split down the middle, with 52 percent saying they wanted to be confident in their feelings and 48 percent simply wanting to set boundaries to focus on getting to know one another.

I don't think there is a right or wrong answer, but if you asked me, I'd say I think option B is the better option. In a world where access to single people has never been easier, deciding together to be exclusive while you get to know one another seems not only like the best way for you to sort out how you feel, but it's also the best way to create clarity within a relationship early on.

Creating clarity by defining where you both are is important at all stages of a relationship, because people don't just wake up and start giving you more than they need to get what they want. Even in the most loving relationships, you still have to talk through your expectations with your partner, and even in the most loving relationships we can take advantage of our partners. We take advantage of the people we love all the time. In fact, our partner is usually our go-to person to take advantage of, because they're not going anywhere and they love us.

Many people want to avoid these kinds of conversations, and that almost always comes from fear—fear of disappointment, fear of conflict. You're afraid of having another person get mad at you, or of losing the good sex. The person who wants a deeper relationship doesn't say, "Listen, I don't want to keep doing this. I like you. I want you to be my girlfriend/boyfriend," because they're afraid that that person will say, "Well, I don't want that, but I don't want to stop having sex with you." In the long run it's better to have the conversation, because let's face it, sticking around and avoiding a conversation when you know something is out of balance often just delays the inevitable.

After these conversations, you also need to be willing to enforce the boundaries you're trying to set, because a boundary is only as good as its enforcement. You can't say, "I don't want you to sleep with other people," and when the other person says, "Too bad," you keep sleeping with them while feeling the same feelings. You can't say, "I want you to spend more of your free time with me," and then never get any more time. That seems so obvious, but a lot of people will not get the resolution they want and just remain in that situation. They'll convince themselves and their friends that they would rather be with that person who doesn't want to date them than lose what they currently have, even if they're settling for crumbs. But the number one goal of defining a relationship is to stop accepting less than what you want.

When you are ready to define a relationship, the most important thing to do is never ask the other person what they want before you set a boundary, which is exactly what most people do. If you begin the conversation by asking them what they want, you're giving away your power to get what you want. It's very hard to enforce a boundary when you've already given away your power. Instead, you should say exactly what you want: I don't want to sleep with other people. I want to be boyfriend and girlfriend. I want to spend more time together—whatever it is, and then you tell them why you feel the way you do.

Then, when you're done telling them, you don't say anything. They will either agree with you or not. If they don't agree with you, you can just say, "Okay, I'm sorry you feel that way"—but do not compromise on the boundary you've just defined. Remember that some people do just get cold feet—with those people, if you're willing to walk away when they don't respect the boundary you just set, they'll come around. If they don't, they never were going to be with you the way you wanted in the first place. So don't start with a question, and don't compromise.

I'll add that after I tell people this, I often get asked, "But when is the right time to ask for what they want?" The answer is never, at least in terms of defining a relationship. Remember that the big thing is not asking—it's telling them what you want and what your expectations are, seeing how they respond to that, and sticking with the boundaries you made.

One last thought about defining a relationship: I think that it should be less stressful and momentous. The analogy I use is browsing movies on Netflix. With dating, we're watching all these previews, hoping to find the perfect movie instead of just starting the movie. But what if we pressed play more often with people we're already quote-unquote seriously dating?

You don't have to think you're going to marry someone to take them seriously. Why not agree to get off the apps, stop sleeping with other people, meet each other's friends, and get to know each other? It might not work out after just a couple of weeks or months, but you'll learn something about yourself and about your relationships, and that's kind of the whole point of dating, right? More importantly, you'll both come to that realization faster and with far fewer of the hurt feelings and worries that come from a lack of communication.

As I said, we don't do that mainly because we're afraid—afraid of breakups and hurting people's feelings, but mainly afraid that we'll be dating someone else when that real other perfect person finally shows up. Yeah, if that happens, it's going to be really awkward. You might look like the bad guy, but you're not married—you're not even engaged. You're just dating. We're acting like getting out of a relationship with any boundaries requires lawyers or a divorce, but all it requires are conversations. But the cost of avoiding those awkward moments and situations is missing out on getting to know some potentially perfect people.

I was as guilty of this as anyone. I stayed single for a long time until I met Natalie, and part of it was because I was waiting to be knocked off my feet with an obvious choice, a perfect movie. But I now see the best way to figure that out is to actually give it a shot. I could have had maybe five to ten different relationships in that time, and learned so much more from those people and what I wanted out of a relationship.

KNOW WHEN TO ASK WHY (AND WHEN NOT TO)

I think one of the biggest mistakes people make when it comes to dating is they don't rely on the word WHY. Why is a very powerful word. When used properly, why is a word that can give us so much more information about a situation, and help us better understand it. It's one of my favorite words to use in life, and even on my show: When people call in to tell me their story and then ask me for advice, I make them tell me why all the time. "Why did you agree to that? Why did you tell them that? Why did you do that?" Once they start thinking about the real why behind their actions—they were afraid of rejection, maybe—I can start getting to the real truth of their situation. And you can use why this way too.

Another good reason to think about the word "why" when you're dating is that people often accept the things they're told when they should really be asking why. The best and easiest to understand example of this is when somebody uses the word "love." We all desire to be loved—many of us have dreamed about it, even longed for it for some time. So when we hear the words "I love you" from someone else, or even just "I really like you," we often get caught up in the moment. If it's a person we feel similar about, it's very easy to just say, "I love you too."

While I'm not trying to be a buzzkill and ruin a moment you have been waiting for, it's important you start asking why as soon as possible afterwards. Yet almost universally, we do the literal opposite—we accept those words at face value. Then a few months down the road, that person ghosts us and we're thinking, *How did that happen?* If we'd just asked why they felt the way they did—and evaluate the answer—maybe we wouldn't end up being hurt.

Like all emotions, love is subjective. Words mean different things to different people. Asking why is a great way to help protect yourself from the immature and the overly excited. The person falling in love for the first time is going to have a different point of view on love than the person who is falling in love for the third time, or a person who caught their last ex cheating on them, or a player. Some people see love as an intense feeling, and others view it as something that builds over time. When you're asking, "Hey, tell me, why do you love me?," you're just making sure their feelings mean the same thing as your feelings.

Imagine two people who are dating and getting excited about one another. One of those people has been crushing on the other for some time, and maybe they still can't believe this person likes them back. A couple months in, the person who had been crushing says, "I love you!" The other person asks, "Why do you love me?" The response could be, "I just never thought I would get to be with someone like you."

Now I'll admit that might sound charming. If someone said that to me, even if my instincts told me to ask why, my ego would just tell me to shut up and take the compliment. "They just told us how special we are! Who are we to question that?" But that's really a time to follow up with another why—to find out more about what that person meant. For this reason, asking why is a great way to help protect yourself from anyone just telling you something to get laid.

Why are we special to them? Is it because you are someone they see as exceptionally attractive, or of a certain social standing? Maybe what they really mean is, "I love having sex with you." But maybe you'll hear something more reassuring, something along the lines of, "I love that you make me feel safe, and you always communicate openly with me." Or, "I love that you help me work on my insecurities without judging me for having them." Or, "I love that I can be myself around you."

Again, once we start asking why, we can get to the truth of what they mean and how they really feel about us. No matter what, "I just do" is NOT an acceptable final answer to why someone loves you or really likes you or wants to spend any time with you, especially if it's in the heat of the moment while you're deciding whether or not to take another step in the relationship based on guesses about their feelings.

Now there is a dark side to why—when someone tells you they no longer want to see you anymore, the first word out of people's mouths is almost always why. Why has a lot of power, but like other powerful things, it can do more damage than good when used incorrectly. There have been an infinite number of hours spent on two people having the last can-we-just-talk type conversations so that one person can fully understand the why. We all claim it's for closure, but in reality, it's just us trying to get our egos to a place where they can at least consider the possibility of accepting the situation so that we can move on. When we are hurting about something we can't control, like someone telling us they no longer want to date us or no longer love us, our egos latch on to the word "why" out of desperation—we go down rabbit holes for why, we ask everyone we know to help us figure it out.

The truth is the why doesn't really matter when you've just found out someone doesn't love or like you or want to date you anymore—certainly not from their point of view. You're not even interested in why as it relates to having a better understanding of their decision so you can move on. You just want to know why so you can try to change their mind. I honestly don't think in the history of breakups anyone has successfully convinced their partner to change their minds during the "let's just talk" conversations yet will all insist on having them. But again, at the right time a little later, why can be a question you ask yourself in hopes you can make improvement to how you approach situations in the future. It's just that time is not when you're still hurting over the fact that someone's feelings towards you have changed.

When used at the right time, and in the right way, the word "why" can be a huge step in you feeling more in control and more powerful, and when that happens you are one step closer to finding what you are looking for.

FORGET WHAT MOVIES TEACH US ABOUT DATING

As I was writing this book, I wondered if there had been any professional-level studies on whether people think dating is getting harder or getting easier since we now have all this new technology. Google didn't provide much help, but then I realized—wait, I can poll my own audience on Instagram. I know it's not a professional poll, but what I found was that 90 percent of my followers think it's harder to find love now than it was fifty years ago, and 91 percent think it's harder than it was ten years ago, and 75 percent of you think it's harder even than it was two years ago.

Logic might lead us to believe that the opposite should be true—that it should be getting easier for us. The possibility to find love for the average person has expanded from your small community to virtually the entire world, right? Additionally, with help from the internet, our pickers are all learning about things like love languages and attachment styles, about gaslighting and love bombing, all of which should help our pickers (see page 39) filter out the fuckboys.

The good news is that it's not our fault. It's just that our culture keeps giving us really bad models for dating.

To help explain what I mean, I am going to talk about the movie *The Notebook*. Yes, *The Notebook*, considered by many to be one of the best modern-day romantic love stories. It's a really good movie, enjoyed by both men and women and seemingly anyone looking for the ideal of finding love. Except that *The Notebook* is just a story about two toxic people hurting others to get their way, that is then sold and enjoyed as a beautiful love story.

I don't think this is breaking news to some of you, but for the ones who are wondering where I get the audacity, let's do a quick review: Noah got his first date with Ali by threatening suicide. The guy hung on with one arm from the top of a Ferris wheel. Athletic or not, had there been a little more moisture on those hands, he could have slipped and died. Then Ali cheated on her fiancé; then Noah wrote Ali one letter every day without a single response. (That's much more problematic than it is romantic.) For anyone questioning that, Noah had no idea Ali's mom was intercepting his letters. In modern-day terms that's the same as someone sending 365 unanswered texts. That aren't just "Hey, I miss you." They were paragraphs. That's problematic. They were also both quick to anger.

And last but not least, Noah was a fuckboy. What?! You must be thinking, *Nick! I have watched this movie hundreds of times. Noah is not a fuckboy!!* I'm sorry, but he is indeed a fuckboy. Remember how he treated the widow Martha, and the whole mini-montage where older Noah-as-Duke said something like, "There was the occasional lady." That is fuckboy speak for "I had a lot of sex."

I am not slut-shaming Noah, because this is a sex positive book. The only opinion I have on the frequency of your sex life—which I go over in detail in the chapter on hookup culture on page 127—is that I hope you do it safely and communicate. But if the movie had given us Martha's point of view, all we would have heard was Noah coming up with excuses as to why he couldn't commit: "I'm just focused on selling this house." "My first girlfriend messed me up." "My friend died in the war." "I can't be in a relationship right now . . . but do you want to come over tonight?"

And I know that at least a few of those wonderful women that Noah was hooking up with during that period probably asked him, "So, what are we doing here?" And we know Noah didn't say to them, "I am also in a situationship with Martha the Widow, who is clearly hoping to turn it into a real relationship."

Yes, Noah is a fuckboy.

But even with that knowledge, the next time you watch this movie you will *still* be left feeling the warm and fuzzies, because it ends with them deeply in love. It is teaching us that it doesn't matter how bad or messy things are, it will be worth it in the end. Except, most of us are the Marthas in this story and we keep wasting our time hoping to one day feel like an Ali. *The Notebook* is a lie, because it wants us to believe that love conquers all, even for two shitty people. In reality, those kinds of traits usually end up conquering love, if you give them enough time.

It's not just movies like *The Notebook* that have poisoned our expectations on how we find love. Think about the show *Sex and the City*, which fucked us up too. Throughout the whole show we were made to root for Carrie and Big. We would get excited when they would find their way back to one another, even when it meant they hurt other people. Once again, we were taught to think it doesn't matter how bad it gets or how painful it is—it's worth it in the end. Except that it rarely is.

Now if you're reading this book, chances are you've had either a heartbreak or at least a handful of situationships that have left you feeling defeated, and a little fucked up. This whole book is about being honest with our choices and decisions, the role we played in our journey to find love, and if we are being honest when we watch *The Notebook*, or *Sex and the City*, we maybe see some of our own bad habits in dating. We just didn't feel called out on them, because we're always taught it was all going to work out in the end. It's no wonder our pickers are off, because we've had some really bad role models.

So, now that we understand why Noah and Ali and Carrie and Big aren't role models and their relationships aren't goals, we can start looking for better models of real love, which I talk about in detail on page 136. Hopefully that can start making dating feel a little easier.

QUESTIONS WITH NICK

Q:

How do I impress a guy without losing a sense of who I am?

By being a person who wouldn't change a single thing to impress a guy.

Q:

Best advice for the feeling of not being good enough?

A:

1) You are 100 percent good enough.
2) Spend zero percent of your time with anyone who makes you feel otherwise.

Q:

How do you get through the holidays when you're alone, lol. (Me not you.)

A:

Being single is different than being alone. I'm assuming you're not alone. Stop telling yourself you're alone.

QUESTIONS WITH NICK

Q:

I'm dating a really nice guy, but the spark is gone. How do I end things without hurting him?

A:

Sometimes pain is unavoidable. But you only make it worse by wasting his time not letting him find someone else.

Q:

Any advice for an intentionally single stage of life . . .?

A:

Never completely close any doors to the rooms you eventually hope to fill.

Q:

If I still care about what my ex is doing, does that mean I don't like the new guy I'm dating?

A:

No, it just means you're not totally over your ex. But that's probably your ego not wanting them to move on, because your ego doesn't want to believe they can be happy without you. They can and you should be ok with that. Because you can be happy without them.

QUESTIONS WITH NICK

Q:

What are the red flags to look for when getting to know someone while dating?

A:

Any of their actions that make you think, "That feels wrong, but I think I could fix it."

Q:

How do you tell guys to stop wasting your time?

A:

You don't tell them, you just stop letting them.

Q:

I get called difficult when I set boundaries. Why?

A:

Because they find your boundaries inconvenient. Enforcing your boundaries often means closing the door on people who don't respect them.

Q:

Guy I just started talking to criticizing my finances/how much or little I work. Red Flag?

A:

When they criticize you early on instead of just focusing on getting to know you, they are trying to mold you into someone they like. They're not trying to see if they actually like you.

QUESTIONS WITH NICK

Q:

Do guys care about the number of guys I've slept with?

A:

All depends on the guy. Your person will accept the journey you took to find them.

Q:

How to move on from someone who isn't ready but admits to a connection?

A:

A connection doesn't equal compatibility. I have met hundreds of people I felt connections with that I didn't want to invest in romantically. Their inability to "be ready" would turn into their inability to make you feel loved and that should carry more weight for you than hearing them admit they feel some kind of connection.

Q:

39 and single for the first time in 15 years. How to meet people and actually let them in?

A:

Focus on getting to know them by asking questions. Worry about letting one in when you found someone worth your time.

Q:

How do I let my boyfriend know I want nice surprises like flowers without hurting his feelings?

A:

If you hurt a man's feelings by communicating your love language, you should probably just leave.

CHAPTER 6

NAVIGATING HOOKUP CULTURE

THE MOST IMPORTANT RULE IS TO REMEMBER WHAT HOOKUP CULTURE REALLY IS

As the modern world becomes more progressive, sex outside of marriage or even a relationship is way less taboo. Of course, people have been having casual sex outside of relationships for a long time now, but we are talking about it and doing it more publicly than we used to. It's more accepted. Along with that social change—or maybe because of it—we are able to meet new people through what seems and feels like unlimited dating apps, with almost a paralysis of choice about who to hook up with. People are settling down later in life, and we have more sex partners over the course of our lives too, with more years of being generally single and available. And while there are still plenty of double standards and stigmas that exist around sex, the social acceptance of casual sex outside of a committed relationship has created what a lot of us call "hookup culture."

But with the increased acceptance of hookup culture has come plenty of confusion too, since many of us are hooking up more and communicating less. Maybe back in the day, it would be, "Hey, I like you, you wanna be my girlfriend or boyfriend?" And then, you two had sex. These days there's a huge contradiction: We're becoming increasingly reluctant to define our relationships in any way at all, and increasingly more willing to have sex with people we know very little about or haven't communicated with at all about sex. And that will almost always create confusion and hurt.

As hooking up early on in a relationship has become the norm, so has nervously checking in to see if the person you have been having casual sex with wants to commit to you. Dating can often seem like one big stream of fuckboys coming in and out of our lives. In other words, we're all constantly trying to decipher what sex means, when to have it, and how to avoid regret along the way. But the most important thing we can do is remember what hooking up really means.

To me, the definition of hooking up is sex without an established emotional connection. If you text someone a couple times over a month to come over, I guess you have some kind of connection—but you've still only known each other for a month. As I say on page 138, I think it takes time to really make someone a part of your life and to honestly define your relationship and your commitments to each other. I'm not going to debate here what it means to be in love or how long it takes to fall in love, but if you want to trust the emotional connection that you have built with someone, then that takes a great deal of time. It's not something that most people can accomplish in several months, let alone after a few dates. It often takes more than a year.

An emotional connection is just as unlikely to exist on date three or four or even date ten as it is on date one. In other words, all sex between two people who haven't defined their relationship with each other is sex without an established emotional connection. So pretty much all sex outside of a defined, committed relationship—one where people have defined their expectations to each other in a way they both agree on—is hookup culture without an emotional connection. Once you realize that most sex during dating is hookup culture—and that there is no emotional intimacy attached to it—you're more informed to make decisions about what you want to do.

When people have sex there are typically two main goals in mind. The first being to have fun, and the second to solidify a mutual emotional connection. If you're going to participate in hookup culture, the only goal you should have around sex is the first one—to have a good time.

SET EXPECTATIONS AND BOUNDARIES ASAP

So, if you want to have sex for the goal of having fun, then you should have sex whenever you want. As long as you're with a consenting partner, there is no such thing as too soon in hookup culture. Yet even within hookup culture, I think you need to talk about your expectations, whatever those expectations are. Those expectations might be as simple as "We're just having sex, and neither of us expects to hear from the other person in the next day or two, and neither of us expects we're going on a second date." Those expectations might be, "Hey, we've had hookup sex before, but now I think I might want to explore a mutual connection and go on a real date with you." (And if one person does say they expect some of those things, then the other person should be aware that one of two parties sees this as more than just consensual sex, and they should be honest about their intentions.)

But if you get horny one night and have consensual sex with someone and don't talk about anything other than the fact that you're horny and that you both consent to have sex, then you don't get to have expectations for what the other person is supposed to do. People like to assume expectations that come from sex, but this is not how the world is anymore, and probably never was. You can't think, *Why didn't they call me, we just had sex?* Because in reality there should be no expectations for them to call, because you had not defined your expectations in advance. I guess that would have been a considerate thing to do, to call you, but they're not dating you.

Are you a twenty-year-old person in college with big career aspirations and dreams of moving to Europe? Maybe it's better to be single—maybe you just want to have the occasional hookup because you recognize that you have too many other important priorities, and you're not interested in developing long-term relationships right now. And that's okay. I think there's a time and a place to be selfish in our lives. And you know, eighteen to twenty-two is the most selfish time in our lives, as it should be.

Some people might be recently divorced, dating again for the first time. Maybe they got married when they were twenty-seven, twenty-eight, had a couple of kids, and now they're in their late thirties. Maybe they need to be honest with themselves: *Hey, I haven't lived for myself. Maybe I want to be selfish for a couple of years. That's okay.* Now, if you're going to be selfish, go and be selfish, but be honest with the people you interact with that you're at a selfish point in your life, and set expectations up front. You can go on dates, but maybe you say, "Listen, I'm going to be totally candid with you. You probably don't want to invest a lot in me."

Being selfish and taking time for yourself is okay, but knowing that's what you want to do, and telling other people, is really important. Yet a lot of times in hookup culture, we have sex with someone and we have no idea how things might proceed over the next couple of days. One person might hope the other will call. One person might hope the other doesn't call. Maybe one person gets their feelings hurt, and the other is now considered a bad person.

I think there's far more confusion and hurt feelings in hookup culture than there needs to be because nobody is discussing their expectations before they have sex. Most people don't say, "Listen, I think you're great. I'm physically attracted to you, and would love to hook up, but I just want to have sex. That's all I want of this interaction right now. And if you don't want that, if that's not what you're looking for, that's okay, but maybe we shouldn't do this kind of thing. If you don't want to hook up with me because you want to get physical with someone who's at least interested in the possibility of having a serious relationship with you, then I'm not your person."

Most people also don't say, "I am having sex with you because I think I like you and I am hopeful you'll be interested in having a relationship with me and I want to solidify an emotional connection."

It can be scary to talk about either of those things—because we don't want to be cruel or hurt anyone's feelings and we don't want our own feelings to be hurt. Or maybe we want to avoid confrontation or just don't want to miss out on having sex. Maybe you think your intentions are completely clear already, if you're matching on Tinder and meeting late at night.

Maybe you think talking about all of this is unnecessary, or awkward. But I have found that most people respect this kind of honesty, because you're giving someone else the opportunity and the information to choose wisely for themself. I have found that many, many people are still confused about what the sex means, because the majority of people tend to say vague things, "Let's just see where this goes" or "I am not into a relationship right now." Even if they think what they're saying is clear, the person hearing these vague statements often translates them into what they most want to hear.

I did a poll with my podcast audience about confusion and expectations, and I thought the results were kind of fascinating. My audience is maybe 93 percent female, so it was mainly women answering the question. I asked how many of them had sex with someone they were dating before they even attempted to discuss any kind of expectations or boundaries. And the majority said they had sex right before having discussions about setting boundaries.

And then I had a follow-up question for the ones who had sex before defining boundaries: How many of you ended up feeling led on by that person you were having sex with? And again, the majority of the people said they felt led on. And I'm thinking, *Well, how could you feel led on by that? Because you didn't set up any expectations or boundaries.*

In that same poll, 60 percent of my listeners said that more often than not, sex comes before setting any definitive expectations. And 77 percent of them said they often tried to define the relationship, but their partner avoided defining the relationship while still continuing to date them. And that's where the boundary enforcement comes in.

CASUAL SEX IS STILL SEX

Remember that approaching sex more casually doesn't make it any less powerful. Sex is a great thing. Many would argue it is the single-most enjoyable experience anyone can have. However, it can also come with consequences. Those consequences can be life changing, such as unplanned pregnancies or STIs; they can be really tough lessons, like feeling used, led on, or lied to. This is all to say that if you're going to participate in hookup culture, make sure you still respect the power sex has to change things for everyone involved.

Above all, you have to respect your own feelings and boundaries. If one of your own boundaries is that you realize you don't want to just have sex with a person if they have no interest in a relationship with you at all whatsoever, then you have to respect those boundaries, and make decisions that are best for you—which might be avoiding most hookup culture.

HAVE SEX BECAUSE YOU WANT TO, NOT BECAUSE OF HOW YOU FEEL ABOUT SOMEONE ELSE

I know that might sound nuts, but remember we are talking about hookup culture, and, at the risk of sounding redundant, we are talking about sex with someone you haven't established an emotional connection with.

Yet so many people decide to have sex based on how much they believe the other person likes them. This often results in them feeling used or betrayed. It will never not be disappointing to have sex with someone you like, only to have them end things shortly thereafter, but remember, you're considering having sex with someone who you have only known for a short while. I get that sometimes it feels like you have known them forever, but feelings often get us to ignore reality. The reality is, it takes a long time to really get to know someone. If you're going to decide to have sex with someone because you think you like them, it's only because you like what you know so far. Remember, feelings change, and the less we know about someone the more apt they are to change. You have to accept the risk that those feelings can change drastically, especially once you include something as significant as sex.

With all of that in mind, if you're going to have sex with someone early on, the only way to ensure that you won't regret it is to make a decision based solely on what you want to do, not what you think it will mean, what you guess somebody else is thinking, or what you hope will happen. While it's still possible to be disappointed if the other person ends things afterward, you can reflect on the fact that you enjoyed the experience and that you went into it with eyes wide open, and because you really wanted to.

QUESTIONS WITH NICK

Q:

Getting a lot of attention and numbers in public. Can't seem to transition to a relationship.

A:

Maybe your attention is spread thin, and they can all sense it. Or you're trying to move things too fast with them all and they can sense that. Slow down, you're only looking for one.

Q:

Unfollows you after you hook up and then you match on Tinder. Help?

A:

You're spending all your energy trying to figure out how someone you dismissed feels about you. Instead, just hold people accountable for how they treat you.

Q:

We hooked up a couple times and keep in contact, but he tells me about dates he goes on. WTF?

A:

He's trying to establish a boundary (in an immature way) that he only wants to have sex with you. He doesn't want anything more.

QUESTIONS WITH NICK

Q:

Can I go from being a fuck buddy to something serious?

A:

Only way to find out is to stop sleeping with him.

Q:

If a guy tells me he's not ready for a relationship but likes me, should I go for him?

A:

I like carrots, but I have no plans on exclusively eating them anytime soon.

Q:

How to tell if they're lying?

A:

Ask more questions. It's easy to answer and stay calm when it's the truth. If they try to make you feel bad for asking questions, they are probably trying to hide something.

CHAPTER 7

REAL LOVE AND SERIOUS RELATIONSHIPS

THERE'S NO SUCH THING AS LOVE AT FIRST SIGHT

If real loves comes from two people accepting one another's weird qualities, then love at first sight is a myth. There is lust and excitement at first sight, but not love. First meetings or first dates have limits to how much we can learn about another person. Lust and excitement can certainly lead to love, but anyone in love who tells you they knew they were in love the moment they saw their partner just has the benefit of hindsight. There are far more people who have been fooled by "love at first sight."

"I know this sounds crazy, but it feels like I have known you forever." Ever heard that one before? It's one of the most common things two people who find themselves caught off guard when feeling an unexpected connection say to one another. Even though we say it sounds crazy, many of us make the mistake of believing it's true. We want to believe that somehow this connection we are feeling is so strong it psychically connects their brain to ours and downloads all the things there are to learn about them without asking questions or experiencing life with them. When you say, "I know this sounds crazy," that is the kind of magic you're suggesting would have to be possible for the "it feels like I've known you forever" part to be true.

I say this because we often place an unreasonable amount of pressure on our relationships in the early stages, based on how quickly our feelings can escalate. How fast you fall in love doesn't matter, and yet, we so often like to hear stories that include such things as "I knew she was the one from the moment I saw her," or "It was love at first sight." The truth is, we got excited at first sight and this one actually panned out into love. When you say to yourself, *Oh, I don't know what it is about them, but I just am so into them*, that is you telling yourself you want to like them, but you don't know anything about them. That might be a reason to keep learning, but it's not love.

When someone says, "I love you," you want them to really mean it. You want it to be more than just words. And love at first sight is literally just words. It's an idea of what you might feel someday, based only off of what you know right then—and what you know is not very much. Maybe you're physically attracted to them. Maybe you like their résumé—where they're from, their family history, whether they went to college, their job, their finances—you know, those are all things you might be attracted to. And you love those things. That's what you're really saying—and that's not much.

Before you think to yourself, *Ugh, I hate that! How unromantic*, I want you to imagine two couples: one couple, somehow, experienced love at first sight. They dated and were engaged to be married within fifteen months. Then a year into their marriage, they get new jobs, meet new people, and while they still love each other, that love starts to fade a bit. They both start to wonder if the marriage will last. They hope it will, but they find themselves having doubts.

The second couple met and had a great first date. There was instant chemistry, laughs, and a real interest in seeing one another again. Over the next few weeks, they both went on two dates with other people, but found that they were still connecting with each other more than anyone else. They both considered that maybe this could be their person. However, they each saw some non-negotiables in each other, and they were cautious because they both had been disappointed in the past. They told themselves they should take more time to get to know the other person before trusting them with their heart. As time went on, the doubts subsided and their connection grew. Three months in, a committed relationship was established. They were a young couple, so they made sure to prioritize their individual goals as much as their relationship goals. After three years of dating, they got engaged, and to this day, five years later, their connection continues to grow and doubts about their love for each other are nonexistent.

Which couple do you want to be? Which story is more romantic to you? The first couple fell in love at first sight. It was instant. They knew immediately that they would fall in love and marry. They actually fell in love, got married, and then it started to fade in and out. The second couple felt sparks immediately too, but proceeded with caution, and doing so gave them the time to build a stable romance. Their relationship worked out over time. Now, of course these are theoretical scenarios, and two people that meet and move forward the way the first couple did could live happily ever after, just as two people who took things slowly could wind up splitting after ten years together. But my point is that our fixation on the romanticism of falling in love "at first sight" can obscure the big picture, which is really all about finding a healthy, lasting partnership.

What it means to be in love varies from person to person. Some people fall in love quickly, while others need more time before they are willing to acknowledge those kinds of feelings. The most important thing to remember is that our feelings change over time, and the less information we base our feelings on, the more likely they are to change. Here are some things I do know about real, healthy love:

1 Real love takes time.

A real, emotionally significant relationship only begins when you uncover your partner's problems, how they deal with stress, the habits and the little quirks that annoy you or other people. Even traits you love at first can turn on you over time. You might go on many dates with someone who's really chill and calm, and at first you really like that about them—that calmness is so different than your last partner. Maybe you just got out of a relationship with somebody who was such a pain in the ass, and you finally met someone who was just relaxed and didn't sweat the small stuff.

Later on, you realize, *Hey, maybe that person is actually a little more lazy than I am.* And that can be frustrating, even though it is the very thing that drew you to them early on. At first, it was really nice to see that calm person, but a few months into it, you start to wish they had a little more sense of urgency, a little bit more motivation. Not everything can wait till tomorrow. You know? Sometimes you just have to get shit done. You could find that very annoying about your partner.

These are the types of things you might have to eventually adjust to, work around, or work with. You might think to yourself, *Yeah, that's kind of annoying, but I really still love being around you*—and that's such a comforting feeling. Some of that good feeling is just accepting your partner—*Hey, everyone has their tics.* And then there's other qualities, where it's "Yeah, that's annoying, and I know that's you, but you still need to work on it." You make that list of things that you're grateful for, and the things that you hope would change or that annoy you, and you say—"Despite all of those things, I really love you. And I love what we both put into this relationship. I love you on a daily basis, you make me feel good and safe about myself. Not all the time, because it can hurt when you disappoint me, but I'm generally a much happier person with you in my life than without, and that's how I know that I love you." And all of this takes time.

I am speaking from my own experience, here. I'm someone who can be an overthinker, I'm someone who sometimes goes down rabbit holes. And when that happens, I can get really focused on something. I can be a bad listener and a terrible interrupter. Of course, I can also be a good listener, as it's my job to listen to other people's stories and problems, but in conversations with friends, or if I get really caught up in my own train of thought, I'll forget to listen. I can't just say, "Well, that's just who I am." If I know that about myself, I need to always work on that. I hate that about myself, and I'll probably always be bad at it, but I am committed to working on it.

Oftentimes when I started to date someone new, there would be something unique about me that this new woman would notice. That unique thing seemed really appealing at first. I could be so intent on something, so focused and excited about something. It seemed really sexy and attractive, at first. But I would always kind of joke that the thing a new girlfriend liked most about me at the beginning might be the thing that irritates them down the line. Because what's interesting and different stops being interesting once it's ten dates in and you're used to it. A lot of things can become annoying ten dates later. And then, nine months later, they couldn't stand it—and eventually we'd break up. I'm sure it wasn't all about one little habit, but these things have a tendency to snowball.

With the relationship I am in now, my girlfriend, Natalie, literally helps me with that habit. Maybe we'll be out with friends at dinner, we'll be in a conversation and I'll get really excited. And if she catches me kinda cutting in instead of letting someone else finish their thought, she'll just tap my foot with her foot. And I know exactly what she's doing. And I'm, "Okay, cool, thanks." No one else knows what's going on, it's something small between us. And she's never said to me that this was something she was going to start doing. She's not yelling at me or embarrassing me in front of other people. She's not like, "God, I can't believe you're doing that thing again." But I picked up on it because we'd had a conversation about it before I acknowledged to her that this is something I tend to do, I am aware of it. And she acknowledged that it bugs her and it's something she wants me to work on. And now, instead of huffing and puffing and sighing at me, or constantly dressing me down, or telling me she hates this small thing about me, she's helping me be better about it.

And it's just a little tap. And I'm self-aware enough to be like, "Okay. Yup. I'm doing it. Yep. Okay." And I'll just hold my breath and focus on listening more. She's working with me, and I'm never going to be perfect at it, but my desire to be better about it and her desire to not freak out about it because there are so many other things she loves about me speak to the balance in our partnership. To me, that's love—recognizing those negative or hard things, communicating about them, working on them. And that takes time.

Bottom line: Being in love, no matter how slow or fast you feel it, doesn't mean you stop learning about each other. There are always things that will come up that could change your point of view. Keep learning, keep asking questions. Questions are like the brakes on a supercharged love car that just wants to go as fast as possible, even if there could be a deadly cliff waiting for the passengers at the end of the road. Take your time and drive safely.

 Real love takes work.

You should be learning by now that love is something you have to build—it requires a foundation of knowledge about the other person. And building any kind of foundation requires work. You have to choose to do all the things we've been talking about in this book already, and then actually put in the effort to do them—learning about your person, being honest about what you want and who you are, asking questions and listening to the answers, learning to be okay with other people's problems after you've really uncovered who they are. To choose to be with someone requires effort, and I'm a big believer in always putting in the effort, in never taking the other person for granted.

3 Real love is not just saying "I love you."

As I said on page 116, I think we have to be okay with sometimes following up on those words too. The first time we hear them from someone we're dating, especially if you're in some sort of situationship, we might feel like the actions and words don't line up. People should be able to explain their feelings.

If they're saying, "I just think you're so beautiful"—that's probably not enough. But if they can talk about the small things you do, the person you are, little moments they've noticed that make them be better too—that's something. Maybe they say, "You know, there was this one time you did that nice thing for me, and I really liked how you did that." Or "I saw you be so considerate with another person and I just loved that you did that."

With my girlfriend, one thing I told her I liked about her in the beginning is that she's really good at being present. I noticed that if we went to get coffee or to the grocery store, she'd strike up real, simple, candid conversations with the baristas and the cashiers, and it's a nice thing to witness and observe. It makes people feel noticed and special, and I never do that, ever. And it's not because I'm an asshole, it's just I'm in my own head, I'm too busy thinking about stupid things. But seeing her do that, I noticed it, I picked up on it. And I thought to myself, *I really love that about you.* Not only because it shows me that she's considerate of other people, but it also makes me want to try to do that more. Maybe I'll never be as good at it as she is, and that's okay. But I really love that about her. It's a very small thing, but it says so much about who she is—and I can articulate it. There's some substance behind the words "I love you," something that I can point to that lets her know I really see her for who she is.

And that's why I say love needs a foundation, and love just takes time. Unless you're a totally one-dimensional person, you need to learn everything about someone to love all of them. And you can't possibly learn everything about someone on one date, or in a week, or even in a month. You don't go on your first date and see how somebody handles stress or disappointment. And then all of a sudden stress and disappointment come up, and you're like, "Yeah, I don't think they handle it all that well." Or maybe they handle it in a way that doesn't work for you. The more you learn about someone, the more you can love about them. And the more you can love about them, the greater the love really is.

4 Real love takes however long it takes for each person.

So now that we know that the speed of how your feelings develop doesn't matter, we can also see that it is okay if the feelings between the two people in the relationship aren't always totally aligned. It's hard enough to find people we like. Don't put too much emphasis on whether one of you is faster with the feelings than the other, if everything else seems fine. We all come from different situations and have different perspectives, so it's normal for our feelings to grow at different speeds. If you feel like maybe you two might be more than slightly off at times with the level of your feelings, have the guts to check in, to communicate. Try not to be disappointed or defensive if the reality is that things are good, but not perfect. Don't turn good into bad just because things aren't ideal. If you feel like at times you might be more excited than the other person, just remember that you might still have a lot to learn about them too.

However, your feelings do have to be in the same ballpark. If one person is really excited and the other person just seems bored enough to keep dating, even if they get annoyed after five hours of being in the same room, then I don't think things are going to work out. (From our previous discussions, one of those two people is a fuckboy.)

5. Real love requires understanding how your partner gives and receives love.

I am not a therapist, so I won't try and define love language, a term that most of us have already come in contact with these days. But I will say that real love is not just about how you show love or you receive love, it's about making sure you understand how your partner does those things too. You need to be mindful of that, and you have to want to make sure your partner feels love. It's your obligation. That's why I like to be careful calling anything someone does for someone else "the little things," because they're not little things. You know how people say, "I just want to do the little things."

Little things could be physical touch, buying gifts or flowers, making sure you have quality time together, even doing errands you don't need to do—these are often not little things to the people doing them, and they shouldn't be minimized as little. Over time, if you minimize them, it'll start to feel like you don't appreciate them for what they are, which is one person giving love to another person. For example, I am not a big gift giver, and I know my girlfriend would not call me overly romantic. But I'll cook or clean or make the coffee before she wakes up—these might seem to be just chores, but they're really acts of service, and it's how I show my love.

WHY EVERYONE COULD BENEFIT FROM COUPLES THERAPY

Therapy has become significantly more acceptable over the years, which is a really great thing. So naturally, more couples are willing to consider couples therapy even before marriage. Many people think that if they need therapy now, they probably aren't compatible enough to make a forever relationship work. On the other hand, many people believe everyone could benefit from therapy if they're genuinely open to it.

I actually agree with both of those positions. When you are in a relationship that already has glaringly toxic issues, it probably makes more sense to accept the possibility that there is a better connection waiting for you elsewhere.

If you want to seek couples therapy to get someone else to do what you want them to do, that's also not the purpose. Therapy is a great thing, but we have a way of misusing or even weaponizing great things to serve our own needs. Therapy isn't a tool to be used for the purposes of just getting what you want. It's not a tool to be used to get your partner to change, see your point, or win fights. It's a way to help you both more easily accept the way things are so you can better navigate your reality. A couples therapist, assuming they are good at their job, isn't there to take sides. They are there to help both individuals find common ground in any given disagreement and to more effectively communicate going forward.

When we get married, we take vows stating that we will be together forever. While these vows don't preclude couples from ultimately getting divorced, there is greater motivation to seek out couples therapy when the relationship feels broken, because two people who have entered into that level of commitment want to avoid divorce. In a marriage, two people in therapy together are often focused more on protecting the relationship than evaluating whether or not they should even continue to be in the relationship.

But before we're married, it's almost the opposite. When we have not promised our partner that we are committed to them forever no matter what, we can focus on therapy to help us evaluate our relationship. In sports, they will sometimes say the best defense is a good offense. That is how I look at couples therapy when it comes to couples who are not married. If two people are so happy with their relationship and see the potential of it being forever, then I think therapy can have a very positive impact for two people who want to learn how to better communicate.

No matter how great a relationship is, it will eventually face its challenges. Working with a couples therapist early on, before there are any major issues, can help better prepare you for challenges ahead and help you resolve those issues more quickly when they do arise, before they turn into something really toxic.

It's also important to note that if an individual in the relationship is in need of personal therapy for whatever reason, couples therapy isn't a way to circumvent that. If you're dating someone who is toxic toward you, then couples therapy isn't going to fix the relationship. Your partner has to accept how their behavior is affecting the relationship and choose to work on those issues independently. Once those issues are resolved—which, by the way, often takes a lot of time for any real sustainable change—then couples therapy should be considered in order to help strengthen the relationship.

No matter what, you're probably better off finding out your relationship doesn't work for you before getting out of the relationship requires a lawyer.

HOW TO INTERPRET JEALOUSY IN YOUR RELATIONSHIP, AND WHAT YOU CAN DO ABOUT IT

Jealousy is something that all people and all couples face. Even the healthiest of individuals and relationships will have to deal with jealousy. For some, it's what ends a relationship, or maybe stops it from ever really starting. But where does jealousy come from, and how can we determine if it is an issue so severe it will ruin the relationship?

I have never considered myself a jealous person. It doesn't even bother me when men hit on my girlfriend. As far as I'm concerned, if you want to buy my girlfriend a drink, go nuts—you're only wasting your money. I'm generally a confident person, and when I enter into a committed relationship I choose to trust. That's one of the benefits of having been cheated on at a young age, and learning to control my ego. Yes, being cheated on hurt me and it really bruised my ego, but it didn't kill me. Now I know that if someone cheats on me in the future, it's a reflection of them and not me. I choose to trust my partner, because otherwise, what's the point?

Now does that mean I have never felt jealousy? Of course not. I am human. I have insecurities, and every once in a while an insecurity is a trigger that makes me feel jealous.

All jealousy in relationships is caused by someone's insecurities—and there are two types of insecurities that matter in any relationship. The first are insecurities from our past, and the second are insecurities that are triggered by our partner's actions. Your childhood, your family, your dating history—there are so many possibilities from our pasts for creating insecurities. When people don't resolve these insecurities on their own or with therapy, they tend to bring them into their relationships. And we all come into a relationship with some kind of baggage, so no one is without at least some insecurities.

Then there are the actions of our partners. Regardless of who you are or how confident you might be, there are always things that will make us question our partner's intentions. Maybe it's your partner liking someone's certain Instagram pictures, or chatting with a person we see as a potential threat, or always coming home later than they said they would. None of these mean that your partner is being unfaithful, but they are all easily capable of triggering an insecurity, and making us feel jealous. One person might not care if their partner likes certain pics on Instagram, while another might. Maybe it's insecurities from their past, maybe it's just something about dating that they have a strong personal opinion on—and you didn't know, so somehow you did the exact thing that makes them think that you might be crossing a line.

That's why it's important early in a relationship to discuss boundaries and expectations for both of you around what things might trigger jealousy. What are your opinions on being friends or becoming friends with people of the same sex as you, and what do you expect those friendships to look like? What expectations and boundaries do you want to have in this area for the relationship you both say you want to be in?

The most important thing to remember is that the other person's feelings and expectations probably won't change much. If you meet someone who you notice is extremely jealous, or tells you that they are, then know they likely have some serious insecurities. Insecurities that have nothing to do with you, but you will still have to deal with them on a regular basis. Even if you're the most trustworthy person in the world, you will most certainly do things you think are completely acceptable behavior, and then still end up being confronted by a jealous partner.

If you are the one who recognizes that you are a jealous person, I urge you to work on learning how to address those insecurities, so that you don't bring them into your next relationship. There is likely no partner who will fix your jealousy issues, if they stem from something you experienced before you two met. Sure, they can help limit how much those insecurities are triggered, but eventually it's going to happen. That takes a huge toll on your relationship, and can create new insecurities for your once-confident partner. It's draining to consider yourself trustworthy and mindful of your partners feelings, and yet still have them constantly question you and your motives.

Again, your best approach is being honest about it. If you're feeling a little insecure about something your partner is doing, then the best way to address it is to admit to the insecurity soon after you feel it, but not accuse: "Hey, can I be honest? It made me feel a little insecure when you were talking to that woman. It felt a little flirty." That has a much better chance of being received well by your partner than "Why were you flirting with that woman?" When your partner doesn't feel like you're accusing them, but rather wanting to have a conversation about something that bothers you, there is a much greater chance that can focus how they can try to eliminate you having to feel that way in the future by being a little more mindful of their behavior in the future.

QUESTIONS WITH NICK

Q:

Fiancé of four years no longer says he loves me but is going to therapy. Should I keep trying?

A:

What is worse than a failed engagement? A failed marriage, Also . . . I'm not aware of any therapist that can make someone love you. Also . . . would you want a therapist to be the reason he loves you?

Q:

My boyfriend is insecure about me making more money than him . . . what do I do?

A:

Make even more money.

Q:

When do you think is an appropriate time to get engaged after dating?

A:

When you know all their bad habits, their insecurities, how they fight, and then you still love them. Yes . . . I'm aware of the hypocrisy.

QUESTIONS WITH NICK

Q:

My friend keeps cheating on her boyfriend. I don't know what to do because I'm friends with them both.

A:

Not worth having friends who don't have integrity. Do the right thing.

Q:

My fiancé cheated on me A LOT, and he lied to me about it. Just need advice.

A:

Respect yourself more. Then increase your expectations.

Q:

I'm an extrovert my boyfriend is an introvert how do I get him more comfortable socially.

A:

You don't. You accept how he gets comfortable.

Q:

5 words that describe a healthy relationship

A:

Acceptance, Respect, Communication, Independence, Loyalty

QUESTIONS WITH NICK

Q:

My boyfriend is insecure with my number of sexual partners. It's becoming a big problem. Thoughts?

A:

He probably won't get over it. Invest in people who accept you.

Q:

One piece of love advice you wish you knew in your mid-20s?

A:

None of these mean love: wanting something, being jealous, being afraid to lose, obsessing over.

Q:

Best way to navigate a relationship when you both have different love languages?

A:

It's not about having the same one. It's about understanding the differences so you can both want to mutually meet the needs of the other.

QUESTIONS WITH NICK

Q:

22 and dating my soulmate. So excited about the future, but impatient

A:

Every day is a new day to prove it to each other that you are. Deciding that you are one day and not thinking you have to prove it every day after that often leads to taking each other for granted.

Q:

How to accept that someone I love is too scared to get out of his unhappy relationship?

A:

If he is in another relationship, you can't love him. You want to be with him. You can be obsessed with him, but it's not love. Love is something that is reciprocated. He's too busy juggling.

Q:

Want to have Sex with a Married Older man HELP?

A:

Just remember when someone else fucks up your world for their own selfish needs that you're the same as them.

QUESTIONS WITH NICK

Q:

What are the best ways to rebuild trust when your boyfriend cheated on you?

A:

There is only 1 way, to give it time. Trust is like your credit history. Past performances indicate future actions.

Q:

Boyfriend has a lot of walls up when it comes to being romantic. How can I help break those down?

A:

I wouldn't think of it in terms of breaking down walls. People have different ways of expressing love (love languages). First thing to remember is to not judge how your partner expresses their love. He may be expressing it and you don't realize because you're looking for something else. It's just as important to learn to appreciate how your partner shows you love as it is for them to try to love you the way you like to be loved.

QUESTIONS WITH NICK

Q:

I married young and 2 years in I've met someone else who might just be my soulmate. What do I do?

A:

He's probably just different than your husband, which feels like soulmates because he probably has traits your husband doesn't have you wish he did. You have limited experience with other men, so you lack perspective in knowing he's most likely just another guy you're capable of being attracted to. Focus on your marriage until you want out. If you want out, get out. Then explore other options. In that order.

Q:

25 and been with boyfriend for 7 years. I love him but society makes me question if we should see other people before marriage.

A:

Be careful not to blame society for something your gut is telling you.

Q:

I'm in love and I'm so scared of how easy it is to be vulnerable with him. He is amazing to me.

A:

Heartbreak doesn't kill you, it just feels like it will for a while. Love can be forever, and heartbreak is always temporary. The risk is worth it.

CHAPTER 8

MOVING IN WITH YOUR SIGNIFICANT OTHER

THERE ARE ONLY TWO GOOD REASONS
TO MOVE IN TOGETHER

Let's get the most important things out of the way right up front: There are really only two good reasons a couple should move in together:

1. You're married, engaged to be married, or have made some other long-term commitment to one another.
2. You're in a committed relationship, and you've both mutually decided that you want to move in together because you want to spend as much time as possible with one another.

Before we move on, it's very important that you fully understand reason number two. Pay close attention to the words I chose. "Mutually"—that means you both have to share the exact same enthusiasm about taking this step. There can be no convincing of one of the parties by the other. No individual should be making a pros and cons list because the other can't find a reason why it wouldn't be amazing. If you have to convince your partner to move in, it's not the time to move in. To be even clearer—either party saying, "I just don't want to do this/I'm not ready for this" is a valid reason.

You are also not allowed to convince yourself it is mutual through loophole arguments. You can't argue, "Well, if we move in with one another, we will save money; if we save money then we will be less stressed; being less stressed will make us happier, and if we are happier, we will have a better relationship, and then you'll be glad you did it." Nope, you cannot do that. You both truly need to be ready and excited.

Even then, it's still risky—because we are so good at lying to ourselves that it's not uncommon for both people to ignore their gut instincts and go along with the idea—because it seems so pleasing or meets their idea of what a successful relationship should look like. So, if one person has some reservations, they should not be ignored or dismissed. If that's you, and you're reading this and debating whether or not you should move in with your partner, now you really don't even need to finish this section—you know what to do. That's not to say you necessarily need to break up. You could be in a relationship where your feelings are progressing at different paces, which is totally fine (as described on page 141), but you need to wait for them to reach the same place. You can't force it.

Now if some of you are reading this and thinking, *Well, my partner always finds a new reason to not move in, that's why I feel I have to convince them*, then you should consider stopping to define your relationship (page 113) and consider things you're grateful and hopeful for (page 164)—and be prepared to cut your losses instead of investing more time in trying to convince them to move in and being upset or angry when they don't want to.

All that said, living with your significant other can be amazing. If you're really happy with your relationship, it's an opportunity to maximize the time you get to spend with someone you love spending time with. It can also be a very harmful thing to an otherwise very good relationship if it happens too soon for one or both of the people involved—like an athlete pulling a muscle because they gave maximum effort before warming up.

I've learned all this the hard way. It was a year into a relationship that was going great. At this point in the relationship, we were spending almost five nights a week together. Usually at my place, but sometimes at hers. In our particular situation, I had a slightly nicer place from being in the workforce for six years, and she was just getting started. Once her lease was coming to an end, she decided that we should move in together—she felt she was wasting money on rent. I wasn't ready. I had moved in with my last girlfriend, for reasons I now realize were a hail Mary attempt at saving the relationship. I expressed my reservations to my current girlfriend, but she took it as a reflection of how I saw our relationship. "Our relationship isn't like your last one, and I'm not like her," she would say. All of the sudden, a relationship that had been going great was experiencing real friction, all because her lease was up. She did move in with me; then we broke up, meaning she had to move twice, which is a worse financial outcome than paying for an apartment you occasionally don't sleep in.

No matter what, deciding when a couple should take this next step can be confusing. It used to be simple—you moved in together once you got married. In some circles that is still the case, but for most of us, this decision doesn't necessarily mean that an engagement is imminent. We went from having a very clear rule, to what feels like no rules. In the space of two generations, the casualness with which couples decided to cohabitate changed drastically. But what hasn't changed is the two really good reasons for taking that step.

The truth is, when it became largely acceptable for a couple to move in before marriage or engagement, it didn't eliminate the rules about it, it just confused them. Instead of marriage or engagement being an agreed upon trigger for cohabitation, suddenly making this huge financial decision became a new barometer for how committed each person is to a relationship. Sometimes we will just call it the logical next step in a serious relationship. For that reason, many couples make the mistake of moving in when the decision isn't really mutual at all, or before investing the time to properly get to know each other.

Very often one person in the relationship decides it's what they want, so they start presenting their partner all those other reasons they think it's best for the relationship, even if the other person doesn't feel ready. In some relationships this becomes a point of contention. Sometimes two people even mutually decide to move in together, but not because they want to spend as much time together as possible.

THESE ARE NOT GOOD REASONS TO MOVE IN WITH YOUR PARTNER

1 You think it's a test to see what it's like to be married to that person.

I find that the most common bad reason people use to move in with somebody else is that it will be a good test to see what it's like to be married to that person. That you will never really know who someone is until you are living with them. There is some truth to this logic, but there are also plenty of lies. Yes, living with someone before you're married or engaged can give you an idea of what life with them might be like, but it's certainly not the only way to get to know them better. What living with someone can really tell you is what a person is like when they are the most comfortable with you. People tend to be most comfortable in their homes, so we associate living with someone as a way to see who someone really is.

How your partner interacts around their family can be an indication of how they act when they are comfortable; how they act around close friends is another way. How they interact with coworkers is yet another way to observe your partner's behavior. Most relationships have plenty of ways of really getting to know your partner, you just have to pay attention. Once in a while we get really unlucky and meet a narcissist who has a second, secret family, and no amount of paying attention would have helped you, but for the rest of us there are plenty of ways to get a glimpse of what a life with someone might be like without signing a lease together.

You can also spend huuuuuuge amounts of time together, while staying at each other's places, learning all the ins and outs of sharing a space with someone without making a complex financial commitment.

2   **You like them better than your roommate and you can't afford to live on your own.**

Another popular reason focuses on money and convenience. That it just makes sense since the couple already spends most nights together at one or both of their places. This happens all the time. It's a huge mistake. What seems like the best short-term solution for you can be the worst long-term solution for the relationship. You can be in love and not ready to decide if his movie poster gets hung up in the living room. Maybe it's too early in the relationship to try to convince him he needs to invest in curtains. No matter who you live with—roommate or partner—there will be times when you just want to be left alone. It has nothing to do with how in love you are or not. It happens to everyone. So do you think your relationship is ready to face the reality that sometimes you two get sick of one another? When you try to replace your roommate with your partner, you risk the possibility of turning what you love into something that you will eventually want to replace.

3 **You want to settle down, but your partner hasn't asked you to get married yet, so you think that moving in is a good compromise.**

Moving in is also not to be used as a tool to speed up a proposal or a wedding. There is a saying in negotiations that it's a fair deal if both parties feel they didn't get everything they wanted. All the more reason why, if you're trying to negotiate an engagement, it's going to end with some kind of resentment. If your partner isn't as excited as you are to move in, every compromise going forward will make them feel they are losing something rather than that they are gaining something. Instead of your relationship being a reminder of comfort and security, it will start to make your partner feel trapped. Then you'll both be trapped, because you signed a lease together.

(Sidenote: An engagement should also not be a negotiation.)

4 **You feel like you two are growing apart, and moving in will force you to face your issues.**

Yes, this sounds as absurd as you think it does when you're reading it, but it still happens all the time. It tends to happen to couples who had an amazing honeymoon phase in the beginning of their relationship. They made a lot of bold predictions to one another about how perfect they were together. How cute they thought their kids would be. Then they started disliking things about one another, and instead of talking through it, they just ignored it. Then they started to panic internally, because they felt that the great relationship they had was slipping away—the relationship that they told everyone for six months was perfect. So what do they do? They decide the way to fix it is to have another magical honeymoon phase of finding a new place together and picking out some new furniture. Except that they can't really bury their problems under a mound of exciting things. They move in and then three months later, truly hate one another, after spending thousands of dollars on a new living room set.

Moving in can be exciting, but it's not the beginning of a second honeymoon phase many couples hope it will be. If you're both excited and ready to move in together, there will certainly be many great moments to enjoy, but it will rarely erase any points of contention that existed prior to the move. If you have unreasonable expectations about what moving in will do for the relationship, it will only make working through those issues even harder.

5 You're bored.

You don't like what you have, but you don't want to break up. Sounds terrible. I know. Still, it happens all the time.

6 You hate deciding or even fighting over whose house you spend more time in.

This doesn't mean you want more time with them, it means you like things the way they are and you're resistant to change. Moving in isn't going to help. Regardless of how long you have been dating or what stage the relationship is in, only move in if you're both equally excited. If your partner isn't as excited about the idea of moving in, don't freak out. Hear them out—maybe they see things differently. It could even be a healthier idea to wait. It doesn't mean you're less in love than a couple who decides they are ready to cohabitate. But take note of this feeling, because it does suggest that you each like your space.

THINGS YOU SHOULD DO BEFORE YOU MOVE IN TOGETHER

If the mutual excitement is there and you two decide to take this leap, there are just a few things you want to make sure you do so your transition goes as smoothly as possible.

1 **Acknowledge the coming change.**

I don't know if this sounds obvious to some of you or pointless to others, but I think this is a big step that people too often ignore. I don't care how long you have been sleeping in the same bed, deciding to share a single address is a significant change. Too many couples try to pretend that it's not a big deal, out of fear of having to question their decision if the transition is anything but incredibly smooth. That line of thinking is silly. Love isn't devoid of conflict. The day-to-day impacts of taking this step may not be significant, but the step itself is significant for any relationship. Simply acknowledging that there might be some friction that occurs when you take this step will go a long way in keeping whatever small issues arise—closet space, housecleaning—from turning into larger ones. You two will be more willing to discuss those issues instead of being afraid to bring them up out of fear that they might end the relationship. When you ignore small things, they tend to get worse.

2 **Empathize with your partner.**

This will be a change for both of you, so it's really important to consider how this change is going to impact your partner. Do they have to give anything up to make this change? It doesn't matter if it's small or if they're gaining something better in return. Maybe your boyfriend gave up his apartment, and he really loved it. Maybe this is a long-distance relationship and the person moving is giving up a lot, like friends, family, and a whole city. It doesn't matter how great you think it's going to be once they live with you, their whole world is changing. So big or small, simply acknowledging and empathizing with your partner will go a long way. It will make them feel more appreciated, and it will prevent you from feeling defensive if you sense a sadness from them about the things they gave up. It's okay for each of you to feel many emotions surrounding major changes. If you two followed the rule of both being mutually excited, then the emotions should be mostly positive, but that doesn't mean there won't be moments of sadness for the things that were lost. Allow space for your partner to feel without judgment.

By focusing on how things might affect them before they actually do, it will be much easier for you to be supportive.

3 Discuss expenses.

So now that we fully understand everything spoken up until this point, it's safe to talk about expenses, which deserve an entry of their own. Expenses are a huge point of stress for many relationships, and it's easier if you understand how your partner's situation might be different from yours. Expenses are much easier to talk about when the only reason we're discussing them is because we are confident that the desire to move in is mutual, we have acknowledged that this big step will have an impact, and we are focusing on empathizing with our partner. The next step is to figure out what makes the most sense with all the expenses that come with sharing a home—groceries, utilities, furniture, housekeeping, ordering takeout—some of which are required, some of which are not. When there are different income levels, we also have different spending habits.

Lots of people would say that you should always split all of these things down the middle, to avoid resentment, but since every situation is different, it would be stupid to suggest there is only one way. One person could be in law school while the other already has a successful sales career. Maybe one person is a teacher and the other is a doctor, and the doctor owns their apartment, but half the mortgage is still twice as much as the teacher is currently paying. So, even though you're not married, you're going to be living with this person, and you don't want to start things off feeling uneasy about money. Start by examining the situation. Hopefully you already thought of this when you were busy considering all the ways this decision would impact your partner. Maybe it wouldn't make sense to insist on splitting expenses down the middle if you both move into the expensive place you already pay for on your own.

Remember, moving in together is about advancing the relationship. That should be the only purpose and the only goal. That means, for the sake of moving in, reasonable compromises need to be made even with financial decisions—even before you are married—and the more we empathize with our partners the easier it is to determine what is reasonable for the sake of the relationship.

4 Consider your future alone time.

Everyone needs space from time to time. When you don't live together, it's easy to have your own time when you're at your own place. Because moving in together is such a big step, many couples want the validation that they made the right decision so there can be an expectation that they will spend all their time together. Now that you live together, you're often together, even when you would actually maybe prefer that your partner be in the other room. It's totally normal and even healthy to need your own space in a relationship. Prioritize having your alone time and personal hobbies early on to avoid getting couples' fatigue that can come from having zero time for yourself.

CHAPTER 9

SHOULD I STAY OR SHOULD I GO?

KNOWING WHEN TO END A RELATIONSHIP

The dating pool is filled with people who don't try hard enough, as well as people who don't know when to let go. Both sides will argue their method is better. The don't-try-hard-enough people will say that relationships shouldn't be that hard. They say that they're good at trusting their gut and knowing when to walk away. Relationships are an investment, and part of being a good investor is knowing when to walk away from a bad investment.

The try-too-hard people will say that they would rather try super hard to make it work, sometimes ignoring the voice deep down that's saying the relationship is over, or that it is toxic or bad. They hang on a little longer just so that they can ensure they have no regrets. They don't want to make the mistake of dropping a bad investment too early just to watch someone else reap the rewards.

Both sides make valid points, and both arguments risk getting it wrong. When we are in relationships, we can talk ourselves in circles. *Should I break up or should I stay? Sometimes they do this, sometimes I wish that—I really like them, but I just wonder if there's maybe someone better for me?*

Knowing when to end a relationship can be a very stressful decision. You know that any good relationship takes work if it is to succeed, so one minute we'll tell ourselves to work through our issues by considering therapy and trying to empathize with our partners more. The next minute, we'll think about how hard that work really is and that maybe it would just be easier to move on, knowing that failure and overcoming that failure almost always leads to something better. Or maybe you can't even tell if your relationship is good or bad for you. So how do we try to work through all these feelings and come to a decision with confidence?

Whenever I need to make important decisions about things that feel complicated or stressful to me, I try to simplify the problem by not obsessing over the small details, but rather looking at the big picture. I have realized over the years that one very helpful way to figure out if the relationship you're in is worth the effort is to reflect on two important feelings: gratitude and hope. Figure out how much hope you have that things will change in the relationship compared to how much gratitude you have for what you're receiving from the relationship, and also how important the things on either side of the list really are. This is a great way to get the answer of whether you should stay, go, or just work on it a little more.

Hope is a feeling of expectation and desire for a certain thing to happen.

Hope can be a great thing. I'm reminded of an Andy Dufresne quote from *The Shawshank Redemption*, even though I don't totally agree with it: "Hope is a good thing, maybe the best of the things. And good things never die." It's true that hope is a good thing. Sometimes it can be a lifesaver. However, as with most of our emotions and feelings, it needs to be managed by reality so as not to turn into something toxic. If our hope for our relationship never grows into the reality of our relationship, that's an issue.

When people are in relationships, we always talk about our hopes—things we wish we could change or behaviors we could fix. You know, "I hope my boyfriend does this." "I hope my girlfriend does this." Sometimes we don't even say the word "hope," but we imply that we're hopeful for something to change. "If my partner would just pay a little bit more attention to me, or not get so angry so easily . . ."

Hope isn't the feeling you want dominating your state of mind while in a relationship. You only have to look at the definition of the word to understand why: "A feeling of expectation and desire for a certain thing to happen." It's an expectation of something that you don't have but want. If you find yourself frequently hoping when you're in a relationship, you're acknowledging what you don't have. It sounds simple and obvious, but so many of us hold on to relationships hoping for things without acknowledging that those are things we aren't currently getting.

Hope has such a positive feeling behind it. It's optimistic and inspiring. Nevertheless, it's an indicator of an unfulfilled desire. Another thing to think about with regard to hope is that it has an implication of the unknown. It could happen, right? You don't know. But in relationships, we often know more than we let on. We know how our partners act in situations. We know how they react to disappointment or anger. We have experienced what motivates them and what discourages them. We know all these things, so when it comes to hope in relationships, it's far more likely that we have all the information we need about something, and the hope we have is really just us not wanting to accept the reality of the situation as it already exists.

Gratitude is feeling thankful for what someone has given you when they are expecting nothing in return.

I also say it's the quality of being thankful; readiness to show appreciation for and to return kindness. Gratitude, unlike hope, helps you see what you have that you are already thankful for. This really helps to put the important and irreplaceable things into perspective. To be so thankful for someone or something that you just want to show your appreciation, without asking for anything in return, can really tell you how important something is to you.

Anything you say that you're grateful for should be something that you know means a lot to you. Something that will be harder to find with anyone else, because it's usually hard to find things that we're truly grateful for. If you're grateful for how much you feel like a priority to them, if you're grateful that they pay attention to how you receive love and go out of their way to make you feel good. "I am grateful that we have the same values. I am grateful that we make each other feel secure and loved. I am grateful that we effectively communicate through conflict."

You might wonder at this point how listing what you're grateful for is different from listing pros and cons. I think listing things you are grateful for is way more insightful than a pros list. If you realize that the things that you're grateful for have been really hard for you to find to write down, that can put your relationship into perspective too. Or if they've been easy, that can bring clarity.

Once you list the things you hope to change and list the things you're grateful for, that's when you begin to evaluate the importance of each one. The hopes you have in a relationship should mainly be to change pet peeves, not non-negotiables. They should be things you want but can live without. The things you are grateful for should be the things you value the most.

For example, hoping they become less messy is nice, but maybe not as important as hoping they stop screaming at you when they are angry. Or being grateful they like the same TV shows as you might not be as important as being grateful for how they make you feel safe enough to be yourself. No matter what, remember that the things you're hopeful for act as a recognition of what you don't have and what you wish you had, and you really shouldn't be hoping in a relationship for too many things, even if they are just pet peeves. Staying in a relationship where you spend a lot of time hoping for lots of things to happen is not a good place to be.

Thinking about priorities is another way to evaluate these kinds of feelings. You should be a top priority to the person you're in a real relationship with. You shouldn't be their only priority, but you shouldn't be their last priority after everything else, either—their family and their job and their friends and their hobbies.

Depending on where you are at in your life, your priorities can change—for example, things might look different when you're a couple in your twenties, finishing up graduate school with big career aspirations and dreams, versus when you're thirty-two and more established. Sometimes you have to recognize that you're obviously one of three very important priorities for your partner, and that is okay. You have to make sure that you allow your partner to focus on some of those other priorities that aren't you—but, by the same token, you also want to make sure that that person does have an appropriate amount of focus on you too.

I enjoy doing nice things and taking care of the people I love. I enjoy making them a priority. I enjoy giving up things I like to make them happy—of course, even I don't want to do that all the time. Loving someone doesn't mean I have to give up all my other goals and interests. Sometimes it's "I gotta get this done, babe." Or I'm going to go spend some time with a friend or my family. But there's always the recognition of my partner when I do that, that she knows she's a priority too. But some people just don't have that balance, or maybe they haven't thought about how to express it, or maybe—and this is really the one you have to look out for—they're just not interested in making you a priority at all.

One last thing: If you do decide to end things, then that is a great time to hope. Hope when you are single. Hope when you have a broken heart. There is so much that is unknown in those moments, but so many reasons to have hope. Having hope will lift you up when you're down, motivate you to learn from your mistakes, and allow you to be more patient when you feel discouraged about not getting what you want when you want it.

HEALTHY VERSUS TOXIC LOVE

As we just established, a good and healthy relationship will have more things you're grateful for, and fewer things you hope to change. A healthy relationship is really about having someone who loves you for who you are, makes you a priority, and encourages you to want to be a better person. It's about finding someone who accepts you as is, but also holds you accountable for your shortcomings, but with grace, empathy, and patience.

"Love is patient and love is kind" is the start of the Bible verse often used at weddings, and I think that's what love is. It is patient. It is kind—but it does also hold people accountable, which is when you need the empathy.

You want to appreciate someone for who they are, but that doesn't mean they get to be an asshole to you. It doesn't mean you get to be an asshole to them when they're not their best self. It doesn't mean you get to ridicule them. It doesn't mean you get to belittle them. It's about having patience with them, accepting their faults, not needing to change every little thing about them or make sure they're perfect. And when they really step in it, you have to have that patience and grace and empathy to consider why they might have done what they did. And vice versa.

I also think one of the biggest parts of the healthy relationship really comes down to how you communicate. How do you fight, how do you get over stress? Are you trying to win? Are you trying to be happy? Are you trying to be on the same page? Are you trying to be the righteous person, to have something to hold over their head? Do you respect your partner? Or do you roll your eyes when they talk? Because what's the point of being in love if you don't respect one another? Do you support each other, or are you competitive with each other? How do you express yourself when you feel they don't acknowledge or empathize or hear you, and how do they respond to that? In healthy relationships there's no winning or losing when it comes to fights. You don't get any points in a relationship by getting your partner to say, "You're right. I was wrong." You really shouldn't be getting satisfaction from being right or wrong.

Also, I mentioned before, one of the biggest parts of a real relationship is understanding that our insecurities and vulnerabilities are not necessarily imperfections but more just—this is who we are. Not to sound too corny, but one of the best things about being in a real relationship is being able to share those things and have someone still accept you. I remember somebody wrote to ask me on Instagram, "What's the thing you love most about Natalie?" And I replied, "Well, I don't know about what I love most, but one thing about Natalie is that I can share my insecurities with her. And she helps me with them, and she also never makes me feel judged for having them." And what a nice feeling to have in a relationship. Isn't that really what we're all searching for?

I told you earlier about how she gives me a little tap if I interrupt people. I spent all this energy trying to fix it on my own, but it wasn't until I was willing to be vulnerable about it with her that I got anywhere with it. It was when I was finally comfortable enough to acknowledge it to Natalie, and she was comfortable enough to acknowledge that she noticed it, and then she helped me work on it. I think a lot of times when you reveal something to someone in a relationship, you almost hope they aren't honest. You hope they're like, "Oh really? Nooo. I didn't notice that at all."

But when I told Natalie, "I've got this really bad habit of interrupting people," Natalie went, "Yeah, I know." That can be hard to hear sometimes. *You were supposed to tell me it's not a big deal.* But how helpful is that? It is something that I do. I'm aware of it. I know I do it. And for her to acknowledge that, and still not hurt my feelings, and not judge me but instead say, "Let's work on it together," or some version of that, that's amazing.

I am reluctant to define toxic love too much, because we live in this world where we all want to put labels on things—gaslighting, narcissism, toxic behavior. I think it's dangerous because we're applying these terms to our friends and relationships and we're not therapists, we're not experts. And realistically, we've all been quote-unquote toxic even in our healthiest relationships. There will always be times when you have to apologize, saying, "I'm sorry, I overreacted. I don't know why I was like that." And then acknowledge that in that moment you're apologizing for, you were toxic to your partner. But I think the main thing is the larger pattern—it depends on what you're getting out of that relationship or how you feel most days.

I also don't really believe there's such a thing as toxic love—I call it toxic stimulation. We just think it's love. It's something, but it's definitely not love. And we primarily get stuck in these situations because we're afraid of being alone, of being lonely. We also often get wrapped up in things that are dramatic, because they're not boring. As I mentioned in the section on dating on page 119, many people are still trying to find the type of "passion" so prominently displayed in movies like *The Notebook*. Except the only problem is, the love we saw in *The Notebook* was toxic as shit. In case you forgot, Noah threated to kill himself if Ali didn't go on a date with him. Movies (and books) like this present fighting through whatever incompatibilities you have as passion.

We also know the brain literally prefers pain to boredom. We will often choose situations that we know are bad rather than feel lonely or hopeless. There have been studies on choosing pain versus boredom. There was one simple experiment you can watch on YouTube: They brought people into a small room with nothing but a chair and a button—no phone, no books, no nothing.

Immediately after that, they left the people alone in the room, telling them, "We're going to leave you in here for thirty minutes. There's the button—you can push it, you can not push it, we don't care what you do." The button gave them a shock on their finger, like a strong bee sting. Painful, but not life-threatening. They knew there would be a painful consequence to pushing the button. In less than two minutes, almost everyone had pushed the button. The researchers asked them, "Why did you push the button? You knew it was going to hurt you." And many of them responded, "I don't know, I was just bored."

I don't know if that's helpful, but here's another way to think about a toxic relationship: If you're in a relationship that makes you more sad than happy, or more anxious than content, feel more broken than loved, and you've exhausted all healthy forms of trying to fix it, then you're in a toxic relationship. It's time to stop convincing yourself that your current situation is still better than the uncertainties of being single. You have to enforce that boundary, and in this case, enforcing that boundary means walking away.

THE MYTH OF WASTED TIME

One of the common reasons people give for why they don't want to break up from a long-term relationship is the idea of wasted time. If we're going to break up, then why did I invest so much time? How can I walk away, when I have already spent so much time on this? It'll all go to waste. This is also known as a sunk-cost fallacy.

This even happened on a recent season of *Bachelor in Paradise*. Granted, it's only three weeks long, and everything is hyperbolic and escalated in that world, but the woman will say something, like "If he breaks up with me, everything we've gone through is for nothing." I mean, this is a woman who's talking about a three-week experience, and while she is expressing her fear of it not working, the first thing that comes to her mind isn't the specific things she might lose if she loses this person, but the time she's invested in the relationship.

People have to stop thinking that any part of a relationship is a waste. That mindset keeps people stuck in bad relationships, because then that whole four years was a waste of time if it ends in a breakup. Instead, you should think, *Hey, I've had some good times during the past four years, and I am thankful for that. I'll always be grateful for those years, and I don't regret it. I've just realized it's not what I want for the rest of my life. Even so, I'm not going to sit here and think of it as four wasted years, because that was my life, and I am not going to regret it.*

Even if parts of it were hard, don't be afraid to acknowledge what you've worked through, pat yourself on the back, feel a sense of pride for the effort you made — especially if you had a toxic situationship you got out of, or if you were cheated on and made it through. You can actually be proud.

Just think about it — after some time has really passed since a relationship ends, you never look back and truly regret those years. It's usually the opposite — you remember the good things you did, the places you went, the things you learned, and you know that person was part of your life and helped you get to the place you are at now. You wouldn't be who you are without them.

The reality is I've had some really hard breakups and I've thought all these things myself — *I wasted this. I wasted that.* But now that they're in the past, the stories that were the hardest for me, that caused the most tears and the most pain, are the things that bring a smile to my face. And not just because I've overcome the pain. Now I have a girlfriend I love and instead of thinking of those as wasted years, I value them as part of the journey that led me to where I am today.

I like my life. I like where I'm at now. Later on, I can even kind of laugh at myself, about how helpless I felt after a breakup, or how it felt like the end of the world. But clearly it wasn't the end of the world; I've had so many good moments between then and now that I wouldn't have had if I had stayed.

My grandma was right: Now I have the perspective to look back and know that the bad times made the good times possible — they were not a waste.

I've said this to so many people over the years — that the fear of wasting time is not a valid excuse for staying in a relationship. I've done a couple follow-up episodes on people I gave this advice to. And usually what happens is they'll say things like, "I never thought about that, that's really right," or sometimes they're resistant, but you can tell they know that I'm probably right. And then? They never take the advice at first. But three more months will go by, and they'll finally reach their breaking point and that's when they say, "I did the thing that you told me to do. And it's been really helpful. It's changed my life. Ending this bad thing made space for the possibility of new, good things."

QUESTIONS WITH NICK

Q:

I'm addicted to cyberstalking my boyfriend's dumpster fire of an ex. What's wrong with me?

A:

Deep down you're insecure she has something you don't. But that's just in your head. You're giving her power she doesn't desire or even ask for.

Q:

A guy broke up with me and he's acting like a jerk. What do I do?

A:

I typically remove people from my life who don't respect me.

Q:

Just ended things with a guy who wasn't right for me, but I miss him. Any advice?

A:

You miss having someone. Not him.

QUESTIONS WITH NICK

Q:

My boyfriend broke up with me after three years. Can we be friends?

A:

You don't want to be friends . . . you want him to be your boyfriend. But he broke up with you so you're hoping for what you think is the next best thing because you're afraid to let him go and can't imagine life without him. You don't want him as a friend. Friends talk to friends about their sex life. Is that what you want? To hear about his sex life with someone else? Let him go . . . the sooner you accept it, the sooner you will heal.

Q:

Is choosing to leave a marriage for the love of your life wrong?

A:

What did you call your partner when you married them? If you want to get divorced, do it . . . some relationships end . . . but you don't get to make it sound better than it is.

QUESTIONS WITH NICK

Q:

Why does my ex keep messaging me, sending pictures of us, but then says he's too busy for a relationship?

A:

He doesn't want you to move on because he's selfish. He was probably like this in the relationship. My guess is you haven't asked yourself what you need or what you have been getting out of this relationship for a very long time.

Q:

Both parties agreed the first few dates were great. Then the other person did a 180. Why?

A:

They changed their mind. A few dates don't tell you much.

Q:

He says I'm allowed to be myself but I'm not allowed to do things that he disapproves of. Thoughts?

A:

First off, he doesn't have the power to allow you to do anything unless you give it to him. He has the right to ask you to respect a boundary he has, and you have the right to reject it. If his boundaries prevent you from being yourself, then you two probably are as compatible as you want to be.

QUESTIONS WITH NICK

Q:

I'm sick of feeling like a backup plan for their boredom and loneliness. Advice?

A:

You control who you spend your time with, not them.

Q:

On and off with a guy for 4 years. We always gravitate back to each other. Why??

A:

Because you both want to find someone better than each other but you're both too afraid to be alone long enough to find it.

Q:

My boyfriend was sexting other girls. He's never physically cheated and I want to stay with him. Advice?

A:

When you make excuses for others who negatively impact your happiness, the only advice I can offer is . . . Get used to disappointment.

QUESTIONS WITH NICK

Q:

Guy I've been with for 2 years wants a threesome and got mad when I said no. Advice?

A:

Break up!

Q:

Boyfriend keeps snapping 2 girls but says he's just sending pics of the ground to keep up his streak.

A:

If you believe that, I have some magic beans I want to sell you.

Q:

Ex-Boyfriend has new girl, asks to see me, things got intimate, said "I love you." Now blocks me, thoughts?

A:

When you start respecting your own feelings, you will wonder less about people who don't respect you.

Q:

Guy told me he isn't ready to date; thought he was but isn't. Wants to be friends. Thoughts?

A:

Be friends with people you're not interested in having sex with?

CHAPTER 10

GETTING OVER THEM

MY FIRST GIRLFRIEND: THE WHOLE STORY

So you're heartbroken. First off, I'm sorry that you're hurting. It's such a painful feeling, that feeling of someone or something squeezing your heart so much that it constantly aches. The anxiety that consumes you—the only reason you get sleep is that the pure exhaustion from your heart hurts all day long. Then you wake up and for a split second you feel normal, only to immediately remember how broken your heart is, and you can literally feel the anxiety starting to fill up your entire body from head to toe.

I have referenced my heartbreak throughout this book, but since this chapter is all about how you can get over this person who broke your heart—and there is a good chance you're afraid that it might not be possible—it's probably important that you trust that I know exactly how you feel. I don't tell a lot of really personal stories, but I am going to tell you the whole story about my first girlfriend, my first love, and all the heartbreak I had over her. This story has it all, a great meet-cute, ghosting, multiple heartbreaks, and a situationship—all over the span of seven years.

It starts back when I was eighteen years old. I had just graduated high school and was headed to the University of Wisconsin in the fall. I had never had a real, serious relationship in high school, and was excited about all the new people and girls I might meet in college. If you're from the Milwaukee area, like I am, you know of Summerfest, a ten-day musical festival that takes place just before the Fourth of July.

For any teenager, Summerfest was your first taste of what it was like to be at a bar. My friends and I were in awe of how many cute girls were floating around the grounds. We ended up meeting these two girls, and I was instantly attracted to one. She teased me about my frosted-tip hair, so naturally I was immediately excited about her. Then one of my buddies was getting impatient, and wanted to get back to roaming the grounds looking to meet more girls. So we left, and shortly afterwards I said out loud, "Why did we just leave those two girls?" My other friend agreed. So we turned around, and started looking for the two we'd just left. With laser focus, we looked everywhere for those two, for at least an hour. Finally, we gave up, checked out the end of one of the shows, and then ran to the shuttle bus for our ride back. I grew up just outside of the city, and to help the people who lived in the surrounding area commute to the festival, the festival had organized shuttle busses to take people to and from the grounds.

We sat near the front of the bus, with the only open seats left being the ones right in front of us. The bus closed the doors and just as we began to leave, someone smacked the door and begged to be let on. There they were, the two women we spent all night looking for! They sat in those open seats right in front of us, and we spent the whole thirty-minute bus ride back home chatting it up. Sarah and I had our first date a few days later, and began what would end up being a seven-year rollercoaster.

As you can imagine, we loved telling that story to anyone who asked us how we met. Of course, we told ourselves it was because it was fate, and that destiny wanted it to happen. It would be one of the many things I would obsess over later trying to understand why would we meet this way, if fate didn't want us to end up together every time she broke up with me.

That fall we went to separate colleges about an hour apart. I spent almost all of my free time talking to her over the phone or AOL instant messenger, and going home to visit her every single weekend. I didn't miss one weekend: Every Friday I was counting the minutes until my final class ended, and I could jump on the bus to see her. Every single time I got to see her I was excited and every Sunday I dreaded saying goodbye.

Our first breakup happened at the beginning of the second semester of our freshman year. She told me she just wasn't feeling what it was like to be herself, and that if we got married one day, she wouldn't know what it would be like to have dated anyone else.

Keep in mind, we were both nineteen at the time, and this was very rational and normal feeling to have about a young relationship that got way too ahead of itself so quickly. Plus, all I heard was, "married one day." So I knew I had to wait for her to come around. I have two wonderful parents who are still in love who met in their very early twenties. They taught me the importance of love and how you have to work through issues. I very much wanted a love like theirs. I had invested my entire freshman year of college in her, so the idea that it could be over just like that just didn't register with me. All I knew about love as a nineteen-year-old was that it was special, and you need to fight for it.

We didn't talk for a month. It felt like a year. I befriended a girl in my algebra class who was from the East Coast, who I eventually realized probably had a crush on me—but I was too busy obsessively telling her about my heartbreak and trying to figure out how there might be hope. My ex eventually called and asked to see me. I didn't even pretend to play hard to get. I just wanted her back, and I simply did not care if we actually should. So we did.

The second breakup happened at the end of my sophomore year, after she visited me one night. I did the whole rose petal thing, played romantic music, and planned what I thought was an amazing night. She left the next morning, and then she just disappeared. Completely off the grid. She wouldn't answer my calls, voice messages, texts, or emails. It was as if she completely disappeared. I emailed her sister for answers and she responded finally a couple weeks later acknowledging my heartbreak, but told me it was best I just moved on.

I was broken—to me it felt like she had died. She actually never broke up with me—she just flat out disappeared. Then, about a month after she disappeared, she responded to one of my emails and told me she had met someone else and that I needed to move on. I still remember reading that email and how truly broken I felt. For all the people who say, "they ghosted me!" when they disappear after one date, trust me when I say you have no idea how bad ghosting can be.

While we were dating, she would always tell me how skinny I was. While I was mourning her loss, I started lifting weights pretty hard. In the middle of the second semester of my sophomore year, I was slowly starting to move on, but I was far from over it. I was out with some friends on a Friday night and for the first time since our breakup, I started flirting with other girls at a house party, and connecting with one girl in particular. I felt pretty good, and we all went back to my buddy's place. The girl and I started making out in my friend's bedroom. Then there was a knock on the door and my buddy walked in and said, "Sarah is on the phone." To this day I have no idea if it was just a coincidence that she called him just minutes after I finally had the guts to kiss anyone else in his bedroom. To me it truly felt like she was back from the dead. We talked, and she asked if we could meet up, and without hesitation, I said yes.

When we met up a few days later, she commented on how big my arms had gotten, and we of course got back together. At least this time I expressed to her how hurtful it was that she just disappeared, but there was never a question about whether I would or should take her back. I asked just enough questions so that I could justify to myself that I wasn't a total pushover.

That time we dated for about a year and a half. I eventually transferred to another college where some of my closest friends and my sister were going to school. I told myself this was the reason I was transferring, but deep down I knew it was to be closer to her.

My fourth year of college, I got an internship at Miller Brewing. I was really proud, because it was just myself and one other girl from Wisconsin who were part of the internship program. Everyone else was from all over the country. One of the other interns was this girl from Texas, and she was the first girl I had ever looked at the same way I did my ex. I was really taken back by how into her I was. A few weeks into the summer internship, I broke up with my first girlfriend, so I wouldn't feel guilty flirting with my coworker from Texas. She was devastated, and I felt bad, but there was probably a part of me that kept thinking, *You did the same thing to me.*

At the end of the summer, the other girl left, and of course, I went back to my first girlfriend. About a year later, I thought things were really going well between us. I was about to graduate from college, got my first real job, and was fully ready to start my life with her. Then one day, she broke up with me again—at least this time, she gave me the decency of a proper breakup.

Again, I was devastated. This breakup was actually the most painful one. It felt the most real, and lasted the longest of any of them. I would call my mom every single morning to talk about it. I held on to the pain like a badge of honor. I would regularly go to church in the morning before work to light a candle, sit, and pray for my broken heart, and to have her back in my life. I truly made myself suffer so much that I started losing my hair and my friends, because I just wouldn't let it go. I even convinced myself that I wanted to change my career to a teacher because that was what her grandfather was, and I thought that she would admire it.

The fucked-up part of that was that it worked. She had been dating another person, but after she found out that I was thinking of changing careers, she popped back into my life, partly because she took me not moving on as a sign of my loyalty and my love for her. We dated for a couple months, and then she broke up with me again.

This time, I handled it much better, as I finally was realizing how crazy this all was getting. Even so, this period began what would end up being a situationship that lasted a year and a half—where she would hang out with me and the other guy she had been dating during the most recent breakup. It took me a whole year to realize that was bullshit, and just as I was about to stop it, she was ready to get back together with me.

Then, a year and a half later, I met the woman who would become my second serious girlfriend, and I finally broke up with the first one for good. Girlfriend number two became girlfriend number two the very next day—and in truth, I always remember feeling that I was never fully over my first serious girlfriend until the second serious girlfriend cheated on me a year and a half later.

Even to tell that story now, I am very self-conscious about how crazy it all sounds, but my hope is that it makes you trust that I very much can relate to your pain. I am not sure what you think about me or about her. The truth is, we both played a role in everything that happened. When my heart was broken, I never took the time to look at the relationship and our actions to determine if any of it was something healthy for me. I just focused on my pain, and used it to justify my obsession with getting her back. I refused to accept that I needed to move on. If anyone questioned me at that time, I would just chalk up it up to them not understanding love.

By the end of those seven years, there was no good guy or bad guy. We both certainly made mistakes. We were two young people who wanted to feel love, but also tried to experience the world at the same time without the guts or maturity to deal with it the right way. I lost out on a lot of moments, friends, and experiences because I refused to even try to move on, but my lasting memory of her is of someone with a really amazing heart and who truly loved the people she cared about. We taught each other some very valuable lessons in the hardest possible ways. For all the pain that relationship caused me, it will always have a special place in my heart. I don't think about it much, but if I do it makes me smile. So much of what I talk about as it relates to love and dating comes from all the mistakes I made when it came to how I internalized my feelings when growing through that relationship.

So now that you've read about all the times I obsessively focused on getting back together with my first girlfriend regardless of her actions, or the overall health of the relationship, I hope you feel this chapter isn't coming from a place of judgment. When we are on the outside looking in on another person's relationship ending, it is so easy for us all to say things like, "They don't deserve you." Or, "Block them," or "Don't wish them a happy birthday."

Whoever you are that is reading this book, I am sure there are many differences between you and I. Differences where we might not be able to relate to one another, but I think we can all relate to love and heartbreak. It is amazing, really, because no matter who you are, who you love, or where you are from, love is universal. So when the loss of love is the thing that breaks you, it's something that everyone can relate to.

STOP GIVING YOURSELF CHEAT DAYS

They say the first step in getting over an addiction is to admit to yourself that you have a problem. Even once we can recognize that we have a problem, it can still be pretty challenging to give up that habit. If you really want to get over an ex, stop giving yourself cheat days.

It's hard to surrender the things we want but can't have anymore because we know they are not good for us. Things like drinking, smoking, sugar, drugs, and fuckboys. All of these things can be enjoyed in small doses, sure. When we have the ability to limit how much we use at any given time, we can enjoy them with little to no negative side effects. The thing about these vices is that, for the most part, we all accept that these things can be harmful if they are abused. If we are lying to ourselves about how these things affect us, then we are not being honest with ourselves about our inability to control how much we use them.

We can be addicted to exes too. What makes exes even more dangerous is that we are addicted to them and we don't even realize that they are harmful. We actually think of them as something that will make us feel better, not only in the short term, but in the long term as well.

With the other things I just mentioned—alcohol, smoking, sugar, drugs, fuckboys—we are at least aware that they can be harmful to us. We also know they have a negative impact on our physical, mental, and emotional health if we enjoy too much of them at once or for long periods of time. When we indulge in them, we accept that there is a tradeoff. We want the short-term pleasure even though we know that it will be followed by some kind of hangover, inflammation, or shitty feeling.

When it comes to exes, we are often blinded to the reality that they are just as toxic for our well-being as getting blackout drunk on tequila. Sometimes exes are toxic because they have always been toxic to us even before they were exes. They manipulate, ridicule, gaslight, and always, in some way or another, make us feel pathetic. They have always had the same impact on our well-being as a bag of Skittles has. You're addicted to their sweetness, which comes in the form of short-term pleasure followed by the inevitable crash and burn, because nothing they did for you was actually selfless.

Sometimes things that used to be good for us go bad. Maybe your ex used to be really good for you. There was a time that they were nurturing, helped you feel better, and were overall good for your health. Like vegetables. But vegetables can go rotten and become covered with bacteria that will make us sick if we eat them. No matter how healthy the vegetables used to be, they're just a stomachache waiting to happen now. The bad part about exes that used to be good but have now gone bad is that it's not always easy to tell that they've expired. It would be like if vegetables only rotted on the inside and you were totally unaware of the change for those first few bites. But the bacteria inside the vegetable would still make you sick. If we knew that the vegetable was making us feel rotten, we would stop eating it and throw it out. We need to do the same with exes. We need to throw them out when they cause us more harm than good.

It's time to stop romanticizing how the relationship made you feel in the past and start being honest with how the relationship makes you feel in the present. Sad, vulnerable, insecure, and lonely shouldn't be the feelings a person brings out in us the majority of the time. When those feelings exist far more often and with more consistency than love, security, and confidence, it's time to start focusing on how you're going to overcome this addiction.

So now you have accepted the idea that this person is no longer healthy for you. That doesn't mean your heart's or body's addiction to them is gone. Like any addiction, we need to get our bodies to not rely on the fix that comes from having this ex around. The more intense the addiction, the harder it will be at first. The more withdrawals we will experience. It's so important not to give in to the pain of not having them around, because that will only delay the healing process.

So many people dealing with heartbreak will wonder how long it's going to take before they are healed. We constantly question when we'll finally feel "over it." We have to truly accept the fact that the ex is simply not healthy for us in the long term. What makes heartbreak harder to get over is making the mistake of telling ourselves it's not.

WANTING THEM BACK IS THE REAL TOXIC TRAIT

The thing about heartbreak is that it can make us feel we won't survive it, even though we always will. When you feel like you won't survive something, you go into a sort of fight-or-flight mode to try to eliminate that pain that you think will kill you. When we are feeling heartbroken, we all wish we could just run away from our feelings and make them go away, but that doesn't happen, so our ego and our instincts take over and we try to fight. We focus on trying to fight to get what we had back.

I've talked about the role of your ego in this book, and there is nothing more triggering to your ego than someone you love deciding they no longer want to be with you, or even worse, choosing someone else over you. When your heart is breaking, all your ego wants is to fix any feelings that are making it feel less than. It's not worried about what it will cost you to make it go away, because your ego thinks it will just deal with that cost later.

Part of this is that after a breakup we don't feel like ourselves, because all of a sudden we feel these voids, a loss of feelings of the security, comfort, and stability we once had, and from the literal void of time we used to spend with another person. So we fight to fill these painful voids as fast as possible. Your ego is working in overdrive trying to convince itself—and you—that is has the power to fix everything. That's why you stop giving yourself the same advice you would give to anyone else in your position.

An example of our ego taking over is when my first girlfriend ghosted me. Among many of the feelings I felt then other than pain was embarrassment and shame. I had never even heard of ghosting back then—I truly didn't even imagine it being a thing that could happen to anyone, let alone me. So when she finally popped back in my life and apologized, my ego was satisfied, because she said that it was her fault, which made it not my fault in my ego's eyes. I could get back together with her and just pretend that it never happened. That our love for one another would make everyone forget what she did, and my pain and embarrassment would go away.

Remember above when I said that your ego will deal with the cost later? Well, the way the ego usually deals with that cost is to constantly remind the partner who finally came back about the pain they caused. Your ego will weaponize your pain into a sort of invoice—often in the form of reminders, jabs, and insults—that it will try to present to your partner whenever it sees fit.

So many of us when faced with a broken heart have done these incredible mental gymnastics to convince ourselves that our situation is different, and that it can work out if we can just get back to how things were, no matter how much the other person hurt us. Why is that? What's going on when our hearts are broken that turn us into the very people we would be quick to judge if the shoe was on the other foot?

We tell other people, "You're foolish if you take them back." But when it comes to the people who broke our hearts, we say, "If we truly love each other then we can get through anything, and I truly love you." It sounds so romantic, but it's such a dangerous mindset, because it often becomes a get out of jail free card for people in relationships when they hurt their partners, and it often causes problems in the relationship later on.

Whether we are cheated on, ghosted, or our exes simply decided the idea of someone else was better than what they have with you, it's important to hold those people accountable. How did they take care of your heart after you entrusted them with it? Often the only way to do that is to trust that you will survive the pain they caused, and start investing in people who don't have a track record of breaking your heart.

BLOCK THEM

One thing you do need to do is block them from your life, which goes both ways. Be honest with yourself about removing their ability to have access to you, and your ability to have access to them. We can always find ways to have access, and that gets us into trouble. We are enmeshed in all forms of social media—it doesn't do you much good to block them on Instagram if you're still Snapchat friends or can see your ex's Venmo. So you have to block them on all the apps, stop following them, delete them from your phone. And so often when we do things like this, we're not doing it for ourselves, we're doing it so that our ex notices—which is why we don't fully block or delete them.

Overall, I'm a big believer in being very liberal with your blocking, as blocking someone for the sake of your own mental health is always okay. After a breakup, it's all about you, and taking care of yourself. But the Golden Rule of Blocking is that you should never block someone for a reaction. Blocking someone on social media is never to be used as a tool to elicit a response, or to trigger someone else.

Otherwise, there is no limit on who you should block—the only reason and justification you need is that you think it's good for your mental health to not see what they're up to or control your inhibitions when you are trying to protect your mental health, when you are trying to move on, when you're trying not to dwell on them or be triggered by them. If that's the case, then block away.

STOP WISHING YOUR EX A HAPPY BIRTHDAY

People look for all sorts of reasons not to move on, and birthdays are one of the biggest excuses we use to check in with an ex. We love to convince ourselves that we are being selfless, that this is only about their birthday and the desire to be the bigger person and simply wish them well. Except what you really want is a reason to talk to them without making it obvious that you want to talk to them. It doesn't matter if you are the one who got your heart broken or if you were the one breaking a heart. Breakups are messy and confusing for both parties. If you're the one who was broken up with, you are often left feeling that there was a lack of closure. Sometimes we are lucky enough to accept right away that it's for the best. But most of us want answers that we think will somehow soften the truth that this person we liked or loved simply does not want to be with us any longer. You don't get closure from having the person who no longer wants to be with you find new ways to explain to you why they don't see a future with you. That's not closure, that's torture. Closure comes from acceptance, which takes time. Meanwhile, stop convincing yourself that you just want to be nice and simply wish your ex a happy birthday.

If you're the one who was left heartbroken, before you decide to reach out to wish someone a happy birthday, just know that it's far more likely you will make their day worse, not better. They have most likely already had many difficult conversations with you and probably feel bad too, so getting your text is only going to make them feel bad by forcing them to take time out from their birthday to make sure you're okay again. That's the best case. That's assuming they still care enough about your feelings to stop enjoying what they are doing to take care of you. Just know that they won't like it.

If they do write back, they are doing it out of guilt, not love. What if they simply are confident in their decision and despite your sadness, they know it's for the best for both of you? Well then, they just won't care. They will probably just be annoyed by the inconvenience of you trying to make their day about the relationship they no longer want to be in. So do yourself a favor and just don't. On the small, off chance this person is questioning their decision to end the relationship with you, well then, there is no easier way to have them take stock of that feeling than to not acknowledge their day because they broke up with you; you have decided to move on because you know you will be okay.

I have also gotten these texts on my own birthday, and I'll tell you, honestly, the feeling was either awkwardness or indifference. I've had people who've written to me, "Hey, I want to reach out to my ex—please stop me." And I'll say something like, "When your ex reads that text from you, they'll be annoyed. Or they'll find it inconvenient. Or have any number of negative reactions." I'll tell them that they're not going to get the reaction they want, and that if their ex wanted to talk to them, they would. So if you want to remind them that you still annoy them, then go ahead, reach out.

Now if you're the one who did the heartbreaking and you're thinking about reaching out to wish the person you left a happy birthday message, you need to stop it right now. You don't get to use their day to pop into their life. You're not being nice. You're reminding them that you don't want to be with them. You're giving them false hope. In that brief moment that they get the notification from you but haven't read that message, they want to hear so badly that you miss them, that you regret your decision. Then they read "Happy birthday, hope you have a great day!" So all you have done on their day is reinforce and remind them that you're good. So now instead of just trying their best to "have a great day," they will spend the rest of the day thinking about your shitty reminder that you don't want them.

If you are questioning your decision to end the relationship, that's still not justification to reach out. If you really respect this person, you will wait. Truly think about your decision to leave. Why get back together now? Think about why things ended and whether you are truly willing to put in the work to heal the relationship. And if you're willing to put in the work and you decide to come back, and, in fact, they want you back, they will forgive you for not wishing them a happy birthday. That's the least of your problems.

In case it's not obvious, this isn't exclusive to birthdays. The same goes for holidays. You're their ex, you're no longer a part of their life. If you want to put a positive spin on it, the fact that this relationship was meaningful is why you shouldn't reach out. They were not a casual friend, they were not a coworker, they were someone you cared for deeply. So when you reach out on a significant day, when feelings are still unsettled, you are treating that relationship like it was never more than a casual one. Give that relationship the respect it deserves and simply let it go, because it was too special to be turned into something casual with the click of a "send" button. The relationship being over doesn't mean it wasn't special or that it won't have a place in your heart. It just means it's over, and you need time to heal.

I was once asked by someone how they can pay their ex back the five hundred dollars they owed them after the ex had blocked their phone number and blocked them on all forms of social media. It's great to want to pay off your debts, but then you're trying to give money to someone who didn't even care enough to ask for it. You can live without the hoodie you left at their place. You don't need the cooking pan you loaned them. There is freedom in letting all those things go and starting fresh. They are just excuses for reaching out because you have yet to fully accept that it's time to move on.

You should know that I've been right there too—I remember spending a lot of time when I was going through my bad breakups when I was younger thinking about those birthdays. When those birthdays came up and I wanted to talk to them, it was because I just hadn't let go. It really had nothing to do with their birthday, I realize now—I just wanted to be a part of their day, because I wanted to be a part of their life, you know, and I wanted them to be a part of mine. But once you get some distance and really are over them, you don't do those things anymore—no one's reaching out to their ex that they broke up with five years ago to tell them happy birthday.

NO, YOU CAN'T STAY FRIENDS WITH YOUR EX

Many of us say to ourselves, *But I want to stay friends with my ex.* That's your ego talking. Maybe your ego doesn't want to let go and admit that this person is no longer a part of your life—and staying friends seems an acceptable alternative to nothing, or an excuse to keep them in your life. Or maybe your ego wants you to feel special—you are mature and sophisticated enough to stay friends with an ex. But ask yourself, *If I get married down the road to someone else, am I inviting that ex to my wedding? Would that person belong at the baptism of our child? Would I talk to them about sex or any of the other things I talk about with my actual friends?* Most of the time, the answer is no. Don't turn staying friends into an excuse for not moving on.

NOW IS THE TIME TO STOP ASKING WHY

The dating internet is always full of new buzzwords for bad behavior that can easily lead you into the rabbit hole of trying to understand why a person did what they did to you. I think it's more powerful to reflect on all the times you chose to look the other way with this same person, when your gut was telling you someone was wrong.

Yes, that person hurt you and that feeling sucks, but if you're being honest with yourself, I am certain there were at least a few moments where you thought something was off. As I talk about on page 116, instead of asking why earlier on—as in, asking that person a few more questions to find out why something felt off—you chose to ignore it all over the fear of being hurt by the truth.

So don't ask why they did it, ask why you didn't pay attention to your gut earlier on. That doesn't excuse any crappy thing they might have done to you, and there's nothing wrong with you investing more energy into a relationship you want to work—I'm just trying to help you learn to recognize your behaviors for the future. This relationship wasn't what you deserved, and wondering why it ended is just you giving them more of your energy and more of your power. So stop it!

BONUS: SIX MORE SHORT BREAKUP TIPS

A couple of years ago I wrote a piece for the women's magazine *Bustle* about reliable ways to get over an ex. I still think they're solid advice for anyone:

1. Vent, a little.

Whether you write a letter or have that one last conversation with the ex, getting what you feel you have to say out in the world can help you move forward. You do NOT vent as a means to win them back.

2. Lie, a little.

It's normal to feel down in the dumps, but letting everyone know it for months isn't going to help you get over anything. When people ask how you're doing, say "I'm great," and say it like you mean it. Tell yourself you mean it. (Plus, I bet your life really isn't as crappy as it feels.)

3. Stop reminiscing about how much you loved doing X with your ex.

It's natural to be nostalgic, but honestly, your ex isn't the only one who loves binging Netflix. If you're going to reminisce about anything, start with the pet peeves and the otherwise non-negotiables you probably put up with.

4. When all else fails, watch your version of *Forgetting Sarah Marshall*.

If there is one flick that provides endless amounts of laughter for me, it's this one—and laughter also helps you put everything into perspective.

5. Focus on yourself.

Take advantage of your new free time to do something by and for yourself: Get into better shape, or take the class you always talked about. The payoff is new experiences and personal growth.

6. Don't rush dating.

When you're not ready, nothing sets you back more than a terrible date that enables you to easily glorify your past relationship. You are probably ready when you're really ready to enjoy the above.

THE INTERNET SHOULD NOT BE YOUR THERAPIST

Most would argue that information and knowledge are some of the most powerful tools you could have to protect yourself. Being able to understand whatever situation you are in drastically increases your ability to deal with it, and hopefully overcome it. And there is no bigger space for dating information than the internet. It is essentially endless. It might even be literally endless. Except that the problem with the internet is that not all the information on it is true or trustworthy: It's the wild west. Unpoliced. Most of you have heard the saying, "If you're looking for trouble, you will find it." Well, the internet works the same way. Whatever you are looking for, it's almost certainly a couple clicks away. If you want someone to agree with you, no problem—the internet has got you covered. It's an ocean of confirmation bias. Maybe you're looking for alternative opinions to yours. Easy, the internet has that too.

We have all referred to it as a rabbit hole, because when we get fixated on something the internet provides you as much of that obsession as you can possibly handle, and then some. When we are sad, hurting, and heartbroken, we are vulnerable. When we are vulnerable, we are looking for anything that we think might make us feel better, and the internet often is a place where we go looking for comfort. Except that there is no rabbit at the end of the internet, it's a wolf in sheep's clothing, because it plays to our obsessions and gets us stuck in whatever mindset we were in when we were looking for comfort. Being stuck is the opposite of what you want to be when you are hoping to be on the road to healing from whatever trauma or heartbreak you're dealing with.

For example, I had a woman call into my show and tell a story about a time she met a guy at a bar; they had both been drinking and eventually ended up at his place and had sex. She described how attentive this guy was, how complimentary he was towards her. She spent the night and the next day with the guy she knew nothing about. He continued being charming and suggested they spend the whole day together watching movies and hanging out, until the day wound down and things began to get awkward, as the reality of them still being total strangers set in. Eventually, he would take her home in the clothes she was wearing the night before. When dropping her off, he said something vague like "We should hang out again," or "Talk soon." Again and soon never happened.

When telling me this story, the woman was using the term "love bombing" to describe his behavior of being overly affectionate and comfortable with her during their twelve-hour romance. She did this because the internet told her that love bombing was when someone shows too much affection too early on, only to have their feelings change. Sure, it was comforting to hear how the stranger had manipulated her with love bombing, but knowing that certainly wasn't helping her avoid that happening in the future.

The reality was she met a stranger, had some drinks with him, and then those two strangers ended up having sex. She was enjoying the moment as much as he was, and decided it was more fun to embrace that moment than question how she might feel once the moment ended. They woke up the next morning naked in bed with one another, knowing not much more than each other's names. That's awkward as shit, and sometimes when we get excited or awkward we overcompensate: "You seem great, let's watch movies all day!"

That's what these two did. Then the day wore on and reality set in that they were still strangers. This was an intelligent woman who knows that when a stranger is saying charming things that most strangers wouldn't say there is no reason to think those charming things were anything other than being caught up in the moment.

Except her ego saw it differently. Her ego was whispering to her, "Of course he already knows how amazing you are, because you are in fact amazing. It doesn't matter that you don't know anything about one another." And the internet was there to yell out, "HE WAS LOVE BOMBING YOU!" Instead of facing the reality of the situation and looking for the truth, she could put all the responsibility of her disappointment on a flaw in this man.

Now, if you're thinking, *Well, that was a one-night stand. I'd never do that, and if I did, I would know better than to believe anything the other person said to me.* That may be true, but if we're being honest with ourselves, there are probably many moments that our guts told us something was off but we chose the excitement of our egos possibly being validated over the bigger fear of being let down and hurt.

The internet has become a tool that just shows your ego what it wants, instead of what you might need. It will take definition of real forms of harmful manipulation—like gaslighting or love bombing—and strip them down and repackage them into something you can use to maintain your anger and obsession over whatever it is that might be hurting you.

That is the opposite of what a good therapist would do. They are there to help you navigate your thoughts and to hold yourself accountable for your actions. They do this so that next time you find yourself caught up in the moment, you won't be as vulnerable to the words and actions of someone who was caught up in that moment with you. And if you are in a true dangerous situation where actual gaslighting, love bombing, and other forms of manipulation are occurring, they can properly identify it and help give you the tools and strength to remove yourself from that situation.

So much of this book is about controlling what you can control about your own choices, because you can't control other people. The internet doesn't care if you're controlling what you can control—it just feeds into your obsession. For many people who are vulnerable, it can get them stuck into obsessing over the person who hurt them, instead of focusing that energy onto things that can help them heal. Your energy is your power, and anytime you focus your energy on something or someone who doesn't love or care about you, you're giving your power away because they are giving you nothing in return.

So just be careful scrolling on TikTok and Instagram when you're feeling vulnerable or looking for answers (and maybe read the sections on when and when not to ask why on page 116 or 128). It's far more likely going down the rabbit hole will get you more caught up with and obsessed over a person or situation that you need to walk away from, rather than help you ask yourself what you could have done differently. It can be a great place to find a community, and not feel alone, but it can't replace the benefits of a trained mental health professional if that is something you might need.

Additionally, dating coaches, life coaches, and podcast hosts like myself are not your therapists either. Don't think that what they have to offer you is a suitable replacement or cheaper alternative to working with an actual trained therapist. I mean, obviously, please follow me on TikTok and subscribe to *The Viall Files* as I think you will find it entertaining and helpful—it's just not a replacement for actual therapy!

SOME HONEST REASONS WHY YOUR EX IS REALLY BACK THAT AREN'T AS ROMANTIC AS YOU WANT TO BELIEVE

I always start this discussion by saying: "I am going to say this, and you're going to take it the wrong way. But think of this as a warning: That person who broke up with you? They'll be back."

And right now when I say that to you, if you just went through a breakup, you're getting excited. But I'm not saying that to make you excited. I'm saying that as a warning to you, so that you can learn how to say no when they do come back. And afterward, you can pat yourself on the back, because it's not easy to do, and every time you get over a difficult thing, you should give yourself some credit for getting over a difficult thing. Just as you might say no to Oreos when you go to the grocery store. You say, *Hey, I didn't buy those Oreos. I'm glad I'm not gonna eat them now, and good for me. I'm proud of myself.*

As always, there are exceptions to every rule. Death and taxes still remain the only things that have a 100 percent guarantee of happening, and it is possible that you are the person whose ex will come back and you'll buy the Oreos and you'll have a fairy-tale ending. But I want you to be skeptical and take my warnings, at least at first. There are a lot of things in relationships that are more apt to happen than not, and an ex coming back for bad reasons is one of them. So I feel that it's important for people to prepare in advance to accept the truth about why someone who broke up with us wants back in our lives.

The toughest part about an ex popping back up is when you're excited to hear from them. If you are over it, you will be indifferent. You won't really care about this sudden outreach. You might even feel a little sorry for them, because you have found the peace of knowing there is something better for you out there, and they haven't seen that for themselves yet.

BUT, UNFORTUNATELY, THAT'S NOT
WHAT USUALLY HAPPENS

Most of us have insufferable egos and the idea of someone, hell, anyone, hoping to be a part of our lives feels good. It makes us feel special, even though that's a little toxic of us. I mean, shit, how many of you who are reading this have ever thought to yourself, in the midst of a heartbreak, *I don't care how it happens, I just want them back?*

So, despite getting what we wanted and the hope and excitement that come with it, yet again, I have a responsibility to be the Debbie Downer here and make sure you all understand the motives behind your ex's actions—the why—so you can make a healthy, more informed decision about whether you actually should take them back. I am not here to tell you whether or not you should get back together with them; I'm just here to make sure you see all of the pieces clearly.

Before I get into the list of reasons why, let's make sure we are clear on something. We are talking about the person who left you. They wanted the relationship with you to end. Regardless of the reason, they left. Even if you told each other that it was mutual, you know they still made a choice to not have you in their life, instead of continuing to grow together. They came to the conclusion that their life would be better without this relationship—and you—in it. It doesn't mean they didn't ever really enjoy what they had with you, or that they didn't love you, or that they didn't mean it at the time when they talked about their future with you. But at some point, they came to feel that someone or something else could give them a more fulfilling life than the one they had with you. Agreed? Great.

Now they are back. And even though, deep down, you've (hopefully) accepted that the relationship ended, them being back is really fucking you up a little bit. You're excited but worried. This is what you've dreamt about since they left, but despite your excitement, you have questions about their sincerity. You want clarity on why. You want them to have good answers to your questions so you can give yourself permission to embrace the excitement. So, what is the real reason that they are back?

They are impatient. Impatient about finding someone new or someone that is better suited to them. I don't know about you, but when I had this realization about the return of my ex, it sure sounded underwhelming to me. It felt unworthy of the kind of dramatic reason I wanted for something that was such a big deal in my life and had to do with my happiness. Sadly, it's true. The reason they came back is most likely that they just didn't have the patience to wait for that other person they believed they deserved when they broke up with you.

We don't like waiting. None of us do. Some people are better at waiting than others, but that doesn't mean they like it. They are just better at controlling their urge for instant gratification. They embrace the discomfort of waiting to enjoy the excitement they will get to feel later. Many of us are not so great at that. Once we start waiting, we start negotiating with ourselves: Is it worth the potential payoff we think we will get by waiting, saying fuck it, and going back to what we were doing before we got in line?

When people decide to leave a relationship, they do it because they believe there is something better out there. Sometimes it's for reasons that are obvious—like realizing our partners are unfaithful, when faithfulness is a non-negotiable. Other times, there is just something in our gut that tells us that it is time to move on. Maybe the compromises they made in the relationship are not as healthy as they wanted to believe, at first. Or they could be generally satisfied with their current situation, but still think they could upgrade. Often, those feelings come from someone who has a very limited dating history. They might be in their first or second committed relationship, and they realize it's possible that there is a better match for them than what they have. It might be simply that they're not in a good place emotionally and can't be available, or they have a job they prioritize over you. Whatever the reason, their gut told them there was something that was a better fit out there, and our guts are often right.

So why is it that the ex who trusted their gut pops back into our lives when they once so strongly believed there was something better? As we all know, dating is hard, complicated, and frustrating. They never considered that dating takes time, or the possibility that their expectations of being single might not line up with reality. The newness of being single has a way of masking the warts that exist in the dating world. Time spent in dating is like a really bright lamp that lets us see the warts for what they are. So we start comparing our current warts to the warts we used to have.

This is what's going on with your ex. When their expectations don't meet their reality, they have a tendency to panic. They experience self-doubt. They question their choices. That doesn't mean they were wrong about the problem they thought we had, but it does mean they often reach for the wrong solution instead of realizing that more often than not, the solution takes time to present itself, and often much more time than we wanted or imagined. Remember, people don't like waiting. When we wait, we lose our patience and start to feel uncomfortable about not getting what we want. Sometimes that impatience wins out and our ex thinks that what they had with us wasn't so bad, or at least not bad enough to wait alone.

The real problem with this is the person who broke up with you apparently never got clarity or confirmation that their gut feeling was right or wrong when they first left. They just got impatient. The problem with a lack of clarity is that the feeling didn't go away, it just subsided a bit. It will probably be back, when the comfort of the relationship sets in.

They might tell you that they were wrong or that they needed to make that mistake with someone else so that they could realize how good they had it with you. But it is far more likely that this is just what they convinced themselves of when they got tired of waiting. No one wants to think that they were impatient with their own love life—they would rather admit fault so that they can believe they are going back to something special. They never want to believe they settled. I guess that's what makes it so scary: They probably believe what they are telling you. They are very convincing, because they've probably convinced themself. Yet there is a very strong possibility that they just didn't want to keep looking for something that, deep down, they still believe is out there.

And if it wasn't about finding something better, but instead about where they were in their life, or not prioritizing you—you have to ask yourself the same questions when they reappear: *What will be different this time? Did they just lose patience with seeing their decision through? Are they actually open, ready, and capable now?*

I hope you noticed that I never suggested that your ex was wrong about believing there was something better out there for them. How we feel is how we feel, and there is always a reason for it. In relationships, that reason often comes in the form of poor communication, lack of compatibility, or growing apart. We all deserve someone who feels just as lucky to have us as we feel about them.

So now that you know why they are back, you have the power to decide if you're okay with that reality. Maybe the break is what the relationship needed. As I have said before, there is nothing wrong with taking risks or being vulnerable—just be honest with yourself about the effort that it will require and the risks or extra challenges of dating someone you already associate with heartbreak. Maybe they did figure out how special you are—or maybe you both deserve better than what you can give one another, and it's going to take one of you having the courage to make it happen.

YOUR PAIN DOESN'T MEAN YOU SHOULD GET BACK TOGETHER

So you broke up. If it's at all recent, there is a really good chance that you're hurting right now. You're experiencing all sorts of emotions that don't feel very good. Fear, sadness, loneliness, etc. Whether the decision to end the relationship was yours or theirs, if it was at all meaningful to you, it is going to suck for a bit. You lost something. When you lose something there are usually some negative emotions that follow, and we decide to convince ourselves that we must have lost something special; otherwise, we wouldn't be hurting so much. That just isn't true—your pain doesn't mean it was special.

I like to talk about the stages of a breakup: First, the initial shock of being broken up with, especially when you're the one whose heart was broken, and extra especially if you were blindsided by it. But later there's a part of the process I like to refer to as "you love to hurt so good." People have a tendency to hold on to the pain, because the pain is the only thing they have left of the relationship. We don't want to let it go, because then it's really over.

I've been in this situation. Maybe this is my Catholic upbringing, where you're low-key told that suffering is good. I feel like I applied that to my love life when I was younger—you know, the more it hurt, the more I told myself that I should fight for this relationship and I shouldn't let go. When you're heartbroken, it's natural to think about your ex. It's natural to reflect on the relationship. It's natural to romanticize. I was holding on to the pain because that's all I had left. I remember my ex-girlfriend drove a silver Ford Focus, and I was going around and being like, *Oh my God, I see silver Ford Focuses everywhere I go, it's so painful.* But now, when I really think about it, I was just looking for silver Ford Focuses. I wanted to feel that pain.

The pain becomes a stage in a relationship where we're afraid to stop feeling that pain, because that's the final stage of acceptance that it's over and you've both moved on. So often in breakups we make the mistake of using the pain we feel as a way of evaluating the importance of what we just lost. In this case, the relationship. We have a way of glorifying these relationships solely based on the premise that we don't have them anymore, and not on how we actually felt about what we lost when we had it. The sadder we are, the more we convince ourselves that it was special. That it was all we ever wanted. We decide to dwell on only the things we liked about what was lost, even if there were only a few.

Missing someone isn't an indicator you have to get back with them. Coming to terms with a relationship's end is far more important. You might miss the companionship. You might miss the comfort. You might miss the fact that you had someone to go to dinner with, but missing them doesn't mean love.

Sometimes this happens even when you weren't even in love. I recently caught up with a friend of mine who had been dating this guy for about a year. Everything about the relationship was nice. It was moving forward at a steady pace. They were expressing feelings of love toward one another. They even felt comfortable enough to start spending most nights together. I hadn't spoken with her in a while, so I wanted to get an update on the relationship. Based on how the relationship was progressing, I expected her to be elated. Except she wasn't. She wasn't sad about it either. She was content.

She talked about the relationship the same way a person would talk about their car, if their car was a slightly used Toyota Camry in perfectly good working condition. There is nothing wrong with a used Camry—it gets you where you need to go. It's not uncomfortable, it's pretty reliable. It's totally fine. It's just not your dream car. It's certainly not special. There is nothing exciting about driving a Camry for the rest of your life.

Then a few weeks later I got a call from the same friend. She was in tears. Her boyfriend had just broken up with her, and she was beside herself. The pain she felt was understandable. She just lost someone she cared about. Something that was nice and comfortable. Then she started saying a bunch of things about the relationship she never brought up a month ago when I was asking her about it. She was so quick to talk about all these things she thought were great about it. What she thought she would miss. This same person who, a month ago, talked about the relationship as if it were a suitable car that got her from point A to point B was all of the sudden talking about the same relationship as if it were her dream car.

She took that pain she felt and used it to justify seeing what she lost in a totally different way.

But what should we do with that pain? Well, the best thing to do is not try to make it better or worse in the moment. Just acknowledge the reality. You're hurting. You're sad. Let yourself process those emotions. It's okay to say you're lonely. But don't convince yourself you actually loved the thing you lost more than you did when you had it.

Lists aren't very helpful when thinking about your ideal partner, but they are really effective when you need to remind yourself of all the things you didn't like about an old one. List out ways they made you feel about yourself you didn't like. Things that bugged you about them. Then list out ways they made you feel that you don't think you could find anywhere else. Do a comparison of grateful versus hopeful. As I've said before, I'm guessing when you write it down, take a step back, and look at it, it will be pretty telling.

REJECTION ISN'T FAILURE, IT'S CLARITY

One of the biggest hurdles we face while dating is dealing with rejection. As a result, we go out of our way to avoid being rejected. Oftentimes, that means not asking clarifying questions about what kind of dating situation we are in. Sometimes we go to such great lengths to avoid rejection that instead of facing hard truths, we seek out advice from people we think will tell us what we want to hear. These people are called enablers, and they often take the shape of our closest friends—not because they want to set us up for failure, but because they, too, are hoping that we are the exception and not the rule.

However, engaging in this echo chamber of advice will cause us to waste significant amounts of time in situations that never really had a chance, simply because we were too afraid to face rejection. So instead of trying to avoid rejection—which is impossible—use that energy to try to see rejection differently. Rejection can cause a lot of pain, but one great thing it can offer people is clarity.

If you think of love as your destination, then your romantic partners are the roads you take to get there. Confusion is dirt on your windshield that stops you from being able to tell if you're going in the right direction. Rejection is a car wash that helps you finally see if you need to take a different route to get to your destination. If you're going the wrong direction, it's much better to find that out sooner than later, even if that means having to come to terms with a wrong turn you made earlier in the trip. Yet, so many of us will essentially keep driving on the same road even though we can't see where we're going because we don't want to find we've made a mistake, or that our sense of direction isn't as good as we thought it was.

Keep reminding yourself that it's always good to know which way you're going even if it means realizing it was the wrong way. No one is going to care that you made a mistake. Everyone is driving through their own maze just trying to figure out the right way forward. Next time you find yourself unsure of where things are going, don't be afraid to get the clarity you need to see if you're on the right path.

BEING SINGLE ISN'T BAD

I know dating can be hard. That's why you're reading this book, right? It can be frustrating, exhausting, expensive, disappointing, and confusing, just to name a few of the negatives. It can also be exciting, liberating, and adventurous.

And being single is the same. It can be lonely, boring, frustrating. Yet it can also be reflective, healing, relaxing, and fun.

Dating isn't so bad. Think of it as a risky bet with a really rewarding payoff. It's risky in the sense that every date requires a certain amount of emotional energy, which you have to put out there, regardless of the outcome. And each date has the potential to be the one, but it might take a lot of dates to get there. Even finding love that will one day lead to heartbreak isn't easy to find. I would also like to point out that it's only risky in terms of the unlikelihood that it will work out. Other than that, its downsides are pretty manageable.

Now I know what some of you are thinking—you could be murdered on a date and that's not manageable at all. Which is true, but statistically speaking, you're more likely to get murdered by your spouse than when you are on a first date. Comforting, huh?

Being alone from time to time, even in relationships, is essential for personal growth and good mental health. Being single is just a long-term version of that. It should be used as a nesting period to help you be prepared for when love shows up at your door, if that's what you want. Being single isn't something that we should try to avoid. It's something we should accept. Like we accept the fruits the harvest gives us because they only blossom once in a while. (That almost sounded biblical!) The point is, being single also gives us exciting opportunities that are no longer available when we're in a monogamous open relationship.

So, unless a non-monogamous open relationship is what you're seeking, I would enjoy the freedoms of the single life while you have them.

Do all you can to fight for what you love. Try all healthy approaches to fixing relationship problems. Just don't stop yourself from moving on when it's time because you're afraid of being alone.

Because if you're not afraid of being alone, then it's a lot easier to be honest with yourself about the situation you find yourself in and the person you're with. If being alone seems so bad, if you're anxious about being alone, if you're tired of feeling lonely, and you go on a date with someone who makes a great first impression, then you will feel desperate to make that situation work. And that will mean you just ignore any signs and red flags that don't line up with your ideal, and not ask the right questions.

If you find that your relationship has more bad interactions than ones that are loving, then it would be foolish of you to avoid looking into those issues because you're trying to avoid the downsides of being single. Yet so many of us stay in bad relationships because we tell ourselves we hate dating or we remember feeling lonely when we were single.

There is nothing good about bad, toxic, or stressful relationships. They are painful, heartbreaking, confusing, exhausting, destructive, and potentially permanently damaging. I am sure some contrarian may argue that one positive could be that you can learn from bad relationships, but I don't need to be hit by a bus to learn that it could kill me.

Also remember that you're trying to just fall for one person, you know? (Unless you're polyamorous, which is a completely valid way to experience love, sex, and dating!) But for most of us, our goal when it comes to love is to find one right person. I think we often lose sight of that. That it's a big deal, and we also need to be single and available to make sure we're finding that one.

Being single also comes with a lot of freedom to be independent, to focus on your career or your children or your family, to enjoy your friends, to maybe travel, to be selfish, to do all the things that you like, because relationships take sacrifice and work, and in good relationships you can't always have everything be just how you want it.

You don't want to give up too much of yourself. You don't want to lose who you are in a relationship, but you both want to make the sacrifices. You have to do activities that aren't always your first choice, and you want your partner to be willing to give the same amount, but it does require selflessness and sacrifice. And that's great. It's worth it because you've hopefully found something great and the whole process is rewarding. The sacrifices that you make for the relationship, you get back tenfold in the form of love and affection. And none of that is you getting to think only about yourself, which, if we're being honest, can be really fun and freeing.

When you're single, you don't have to worry about that. You can meet multiple people. You don't have to check in. You can randomly DM someone—there's a lot of freedom in that. And I think people just need to try to embrace it and stop worrying about being single. So "single" is not a bad word. Plus, it's part of the path to one of the best things in the world: Happily ever after.

Well, that's all I have to say for now. I hope you found something in this book that will be helpful. More importantly, keep in mind that everything in this book sounds simple in theory but is challenging in practice. So remember to give yourself a break from time to time. Remember to pat yourself on the back anytime you are honest with yourself about a situation, or anytime you say no to validating your ego over what's best for your heart.

QUESTIONS WITH NICK

Q:

I need closure after a six-year relationship, but my ex won't talk to me. Help?

A:

Write a letter to them and express yourself. Don't expect a response. Truth is, you don't need to talk. You just need to get shit out. Nothing you talk to them about will change anything. So, get it, accept the present, and be hopeful for the future.

Q:

How to move on from your ex when it seems impossible because it's so comfortable :/

A:

Comfort is nice. It's also a crutch. Sometimes we have gotten comfortable with being unhappy. Great things can come from discomfort.

Q:

Can't get over ex. It's been six months but he constantly gaslights me.

A:

He's your ex. Stop letting him have so much power. He can't gaslight you if he's not in your life. You can't get over him because you won't say goodbye.

QUESTIONS WITH NICK

Q:

How to get over a guy who bailed on me 4 times then ghosted me?

A:

You're not thinking about what you want from others. You just want to be enough for them. As soon as you increase your expectations of what you deserve, you will find that behavior unattractive.

Q:

Can't stop thinking about texting my ex when I know it clearly needs to be over, help!

A:

Assume every time you reach out, they respect you less and less.

Q:

How often is too often to talk to an ex?

A:

Anytime you're trying to hold on to something you have already said goodbye to is too many.

QUESTIONS WITH NICK

Q:

SOS, should you get dinner with an ex that WRECKED you but you're pretty sure there's potential?

A:

You're still counting on them for validation, and they still consider you a backup plan. That's not potential, that's holding each other back.

Q:

How do I stop missing an ex after a breakup?

A:

The more you invest in yourself the less time you will have to waste your energy on things that held you back. Like your ex.

Q:

Should I tell my recent ex he was emotionally/verbally abusive or just move on?

A:

It's not your job to fix them. It's your job to protect yourself. Don't give villains access to your worth.

QUESTIONS WITH NICK

Q:

In a happy relationship. Ex is getting married this weekend and can't stop thinking about it. Why?

A:

They are beating you in a race that doesn't matter.

Q:

Do you believe in closure?

A:

Yes, but only in giving closure to yourself. Most people's version of closure is motivated by their egos to hear the "why" from their ex that won't make a difference. Yes, it's nice to get a sincere apology but it's not needed to move on and usually doesn't really come until much later. Well after you stop caring.

Q:

How is the best way to get closure with your ego being involved?

A:

Accepting that someone not wanting to be with you anymore is reason enough to know you shouldn't be in a relationship with them. Because you deserve someone who does. That it's not a reflection of your value as a person or an indication of how future relationships will go. Focus on what you can change and improve in yourself for future partners. Don't obsess over what your partner did or didn't do and equate that to your sense of self-worth.

QUESTIONS WITH NICK

Q:

I can't get over my ex. How do I trust that if it's meant to be it will somehow?

A:

Part of why you can't get over them is embedded in your question. You wanting to trust that if things are meant to be they will be somehow is you holding on to hope. Hope is meant for the future and acceptance helps you let go of the past. Focus on accepting that it's over and be hopeful of finding a love that you deserve instead of trying to force something that you want.

Q:

Ex and I are godparents to the same child. Not on good terms. How do I deal with encounters?

A:

You don't need to be co-godparents at the same time. You're probably using this as an excuse to keep them in your life.

WHAT DOES IT MEAN WHEN THEY SAY . . . ?

"I LIKE YOU, BUT . . ."

When someone says, "I like you" and the next word out of their mouth is "BUT," then 100 percent of the time what they are really saying is that they don't like you enough—to do whatever thing you are talking about. Usually that thing is committing to you in an exclusive relationship. Another common situation that happens is in long-distance relationships when someone says, "I like everything about you, but I just don't do long distance." They might even say they love everything about you, but will say they just have a rule about not doing long-distance relationships. As the saying goes, rules are meant to be broken, and the rules people make for themselves aren't really rules at all; they are just boundaries they created to protect themselves from challenging situations. Everyone makes exceptions to their rules when they want something enough. They push their boundaries to accommodate the things they desire most. So many people make sacrifices for the things they want most in their lives, and those sacrifices help them measure how significant something is to them. It's important to note that when someone says, "I like you but," they aren't lying about the fact that they like you. They do like you, just not enough. Sure, they could say it in a way that hits harder, but it's not their words that are confusing you; it's your ego. Your ego is just focusing on the "I like you" part, then stops listening when they say "but." The "BUT" is very important. You should pay very close attention to any words following a "but" because it's how someone really feels.

"I DON'T WANT TO DO THIS TO YOU"

When someone says, "I don't want to do this to you," what they really mean is "I don't want to do this with you." One of the greatest things about being in love, and having a partner you can trust, is that they will help you through whatever challenges you face. We are pretty selfish people, and most of us are guilty of asking a lot of the people we care about the most. That can be hard in a relationship—but when someone you have been dating says, "I don't want to do this to you," they aren't thinking of your feelings and trying to remove the burden on you. It isn't a cry for help. They're just being a fuckboy, spending time with you when they want sex or are bored—but when you bring up a relationship or wanting more, this is their excuse.

THEY WANT TO "LAY LOW"

When somebody says they want to lay low, and then suggests hanging out alone at either of your places, they are just hoping to hook up. I don't think this is all that shocking for most people, but it's a good reminder for people who want to set boundaries around sex. There is nothing wrong with a guy trying to create an environment that makes it easier to get physical if there is a mutual interest. It's also awkward to say, "Hey, do you want to come over and pretend to watch a movie so we can have sex?" They try to suggest situations that make it easier for both of you. You should, however, be wary of people who do this yet insist their intentions aren't to hook up. If someone says, "I just don't want to be around other people, I want to get to know you," they are probably being misleading about their intentions. There are plenty of public places that are low key and don't have a lot of other people around distracting you from good conversation.

"I NEED SOME TIME TO FIGURE THINGS OUT"

First, I'm not talking about people who are legitimately struggling with depression or a mental health crisis—they of course need to take care of themselves. I'm referring to people who use this excuse when they're really just considering their options. They're putting you on hold while they look for something better. You know how it is when you're shopping and you see something that you think you want, but you're just not sure about it. Maybe it's out of your price range. Maybe you just crave the feeling of buying something, but you know deep down you won't use it or wear it. Well, that's how this person feels about you. They're not totally sold on having or not having you. They want to keep shopping. They ask if they can put you on hold and try to extend the amount of time before they have to put the money down.

Maybe they're not even aware they're not really interested in a relationship with you, but they show they aren't with these vague and cryptic details about their intentions, which you then mistakenly interpret as hope. I mean, taking a break to "figure things out" sounds nice. It sounds like the person you want to be with really wants to put in the extra work to improve their lives—to apply to school or get a new job. Except the only thing they are trying to figure out is if they can do better than you, or just simply if they like you enough to keep investing their time. Think about it—if you had something in your life you needed to figure out that actually had nothing to do with a relationship, wouldn't it be great to have someone you love (or even like) by your side to help you through it?

So what do you do with that information? You don't automatically have to end things in this situation. Just be honest with yourself about what's going on. Maybe the luxury item that stores refuse to put on hold because the supply is too limited and the demand is just too high. And of course, if someone else wants to swoop in and take the luxury item home, well then, that's just the first reluctant buyer's loss. The point is, if they want to consider their options, you can at least also consider your options while you wait. Make yourself available, see what else is out there. Three things could happen: You find another person who makes you happy, the first person rushes back, or the first person doesn't care at all. The important thing is really that you get clarity, which may sting in the short run, but at the end of the day is what you're really seeking.

"LIKE," ON YOUR SOCIAL MEDIA

What does it mean when an ex looks at your social media? The short answer is that it means nothing. The longer answer is that they are bored enough to reminisce about the past. Almost all experiences have the opportunity to be good memories, so just because you might be on their mind doesn't mean they are looking for anything more than an update. If they missed you, they would reach out to you.

THEY "WANT TO TAKE A BREAK"

It means they want to test the waters of single life. There is a good bet that they want to talk to, and probably be physically intimate with, other people without being labeled a cheater. They are hoping to work out the kinks of the single life before they break up to ensure it's safe to do so. The most important thing to know when your partner suggests taking a break is that the break is 100 percent for them; it has nothing to do with helping the relationship. Still, they will probably try to convince you that this break will somehow have a positive effect on the relationship.

What should you do if your partner suggests taking a break? Well, given that your partner already has one foot out the door, the only thing you can really do is give them exactly what they asked for, and more than they bargained for. It takes a lot for someone to bring up taking a break with their partner, so if they bring it up, they have already thought about it a lot and have decided that it's what they want to do. The good news, if there is any, is that they are somewhat hesitant about altogether ending things, so you have to quickly give them a glimpse of what life would be like without you.

Step 1. Stay calm. I know this will be hard, but it's so important. Calmly say that it's not what you want and why. Don't argue and don't try to convince them, just explain how you feel. This won't change their mind, but for your peace of mind, it's important to state how you feel.

Step 2. Once they confirm that they still think it's best, say okay, and immediately start taking advantage of the break. Again, remain calm as fuck. Then, immediately get on every dating app possible. Don't tell them. It's best not to even talk to them. Don't threaten them. Just do it. Start swiping and talking to as many people as possible. If you want to be petty, post something on social media asking for suggestions on the best dating apps and fun places to meet new people.

If your former partner gets mad about you doing exactly what they wanted, just remind them that you didn't want this. You don't want to get any more petty than that. You want to take the high road. Always be calm about giving them exactly want they want. I know this might be hard because you're probably hurt and not wanting to date anyone else, but finding the strength to stay calm and start getting out there is the only way you will remind them of what they're considering letting go. And you might also enjoy this space you thought you didn't want.

THEY "DON'T WANT A RELATIONSHIP," BUT REALLY ACT LIKE THEY DO

All over this book I have referenced the importance of evaluating people's actions over their words. I have gone on and on about how it's easy to say something, but requires much more effort and commitment to show up. I stand by this. However, there is one major exception to this rule: When someone says, "I don't want a relationship" or "I'm not looking for relationship," but their actions make it seem like they actually do. In that instance you should always, and I mean 100 percent of the time, believe this person's words over their actions.

Despite what your friends are telling you, they are not playing hard to get. They are not scared. They are literally telling you that they don't want to date you.

The confusion comes when they then reach out to "see how you're doing." It's not because they're second-guessing what they said. They haven't finally worked up the courage to face the fears they don't even have. They are probably bored. Or horny. Most importantly, they think that they're already setting boundaries by letting you know that they don't want to date you. Since they enjoy your company, hanging out with you is better than being alone, so that's what they're going to do.

Yes, they ask you to dinner on the regular. You spend most of your time with each other. You even still have sex. I agree, based on those three things alone it sounds like you're in a relationship, or on your way to being in a relationship. Except they simply see it as enjoying your company, full stop. It's fun. It's a good time. It's easy. It's comfortable. It's better than being alone. But in their mind, they're thinking that you know what's up, because they already said they didn't want a relationship.

I'm sure that for some of you reading this, that will sting a bit. You've been investing your time, your feelings have grown, and now you're being forced to come to terms with that fact that nothing has changed—or will change—for them. You might even feel anger toward them for having "wasted your time."

But before you direct all that anger their way, make sure to consider the role you played in this.

It took two to create this situation. You were inconsiderate of your own feelings the first time you agreed to invest any more time in them after they said that they did not want to be in a relationship with you.

You can argue that they have been inconsiderate for assuming you were incapable of deciding for yourself whether or not you could handle spending time with them on these terms. And yes, they are certainly demonstrating some selfishness by leading you on with actions that don't align with their words. If you've made it clear that you want and expect more from the situation, then the right thing for the other person to do would have been to walk away. But you also have the power to walk away.

This book isn't about how you can win an argument with a person who doesn't want to commit—it's about helping you control what you can control. You took a risk by continuing to see this person, despite the boundary they put up. That part is on you.

And learning that lesson, even a few times, is okay, but the key is to really learn from it and to eventually be able to sidestep the part where you waste your time and energy. Your gut told you it was a bad idea, and you did it anyway. So next time they say they don't want a relationship, believe them and hang out with them at your own risk.

"I'M SCARED" / "I NEED TO BE ALONE RIGHT NOW" / "IT'S JUST NOT THE RIGHT TIME" / "I'M NOT READY" / "I DON'T KNOW IF IT'S A GOOD IDEA"

Let's say you're hanging out with someone—you're having sex with them. And you say, "I want to date you." The other person says one of the above statements. They're literally telling you they're a fuckboy, and that they don't want to date you. There's something about you that doesn't make them want to make sacrifices—you're not a priority.

QUESTIONS WITH NICK

Q:

I hung out with this guy, we had a good time, laughing and everything. Then all of a sudden

A:

I'll finish the sentence . . . He started to have a good time and laugh with someone else. You will be fine.

Q:

A guy that said he liked me stopped texting me . . . why?

A:

He stopped liking you?

Q:

Guy I dated checked all the boxes but wasn't feeling it so ended it. Fear of commitment?

A:

Or he just doesn't like you. We have to stop making excuses for our egos. Your guy is out there.

Q:

What does it mean when your crush is snapping their fingers at you surprisingly?

A:

That you have become obsessed and looking for any sign that isn't there.

ACKNOWLEDGMENTS

To my parents: I always felt proud to be your son and incredibly lucky to have you has my parents. Thank you for always being there for me when my heart was breaking.

To anyone who I have ever loved: Thank you for being a part of my life and helping me be the person I am today.

To the one I love now: Thank you for being my biggest cheerleader! Having someone who believes in you like you believe in me is a gift I'll always cherish.

To my team: Thank you! I know I can be a pain in the ass.

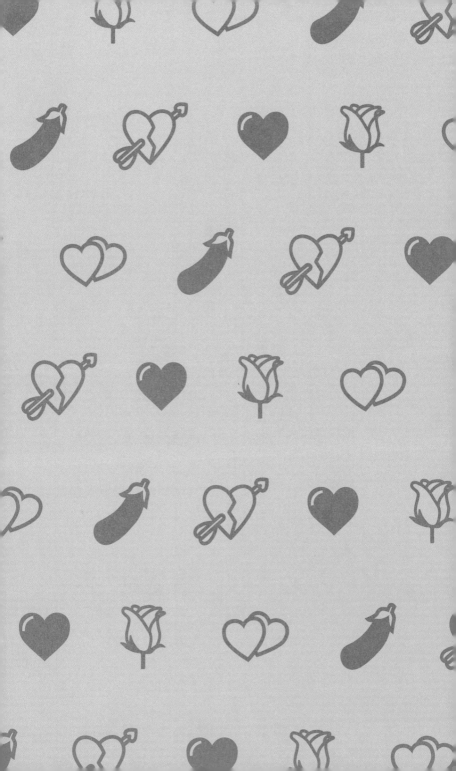

Q:

Is the right person the person who will make u better or just accept u as u?

A:

It's the person who accepts you for who you are but holds you accountable for your weaknesses with grace, empathy, and support.

Q:

What does it mean if you keep making bad decisions about dating people?!

A:

It means you're normal.

Q:

How to get over a difficult breakup with a mama's boy?

A:

Be careful not to make excuses for him by blaming his mom. At the end of the day, he's an adult, and his mom isn't an excuse for him to still be acting like a boy.

Q:

Is getting back together with an ex really that bad if things were healthy & you've both improved?

A:

If it was so healthy you would have worked through issues without having to break up.